Treasures

A Reading/Language Arts Program

Macmillan McGraw-Hill

Contributors

Time Magazine, Accelerated Reader

learning through listening

Students with print disabilities may be eligible to obtain an accessible, audio version of the pupil edition of this textbook. Please call Recording for the Blind & Dyslexic at 1-800-221-4792 for complete information.

A

The *McGraw·Hill* Companies

Macmillan McGraw-Hill

Published by Macmillan/McGraw-Hill, of McGraw-Hill Education, a division of The McGraw-Hill Companies, Inc., Two Penn Plaza, New York, New York 10121.

Printed in the United States of America

ISBN-13: 978-0-02-198812-9/3, Bk. 2
ISBN-10: 0-02-198812-9/3, Bk. 2
1 2 3 4 5 6 7 8 9 (079/043) 11 10 09 08 07

Treasures

A Reading/Language Arts Program

Program Authors

Donald R. Bear
Janice A. Dole
Jana Echevarria
Jan E. Hasbrouck
Scott G. Paris
Timothy Shanahan
Josefina V. Tinajero

**Macmillan
McGraw-Hill**

Unit 4

Determination

Award Winning Selection

THEME: What's Cooking?

Award Winning Selection

THEME: Getting Along

TIME FOR KIDS

THEME: Protecting Our Natural Resources

Challenges

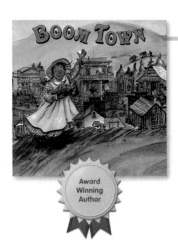

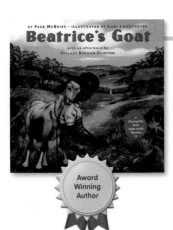

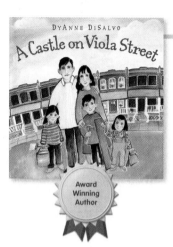

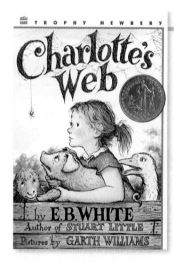

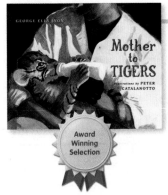

What's Cooking?

Talk About It

What is one meal you would love to learn how to make?

LOG ON Find out more about cooking at **www.macmillanmh.com**

Red and Her Friends

by Marilyn MacGregor

A hen named Red lived in a city. Red and her pals did everything together. One day, Red and her feline friend Fiona went shopping. As they passed a trash-filled, weed-covered lot, Red smiled. "Wouldn't that lot be a **magnificent** spot for a garden?" she asked.

"Have you lost your marbles?" Fiona meowed, looking at Red like she was crazy. "It's a disaster!"

"We'd have to clean it up, of course," said Red. She called Ricardo over and asked for help.

"Sorry. I have a dentist appointment," Ricardo barked and walked away wagging his tail.

Red was disappointed. Fiona stomped her paws angrily.

12

"I'll help you," said Fiona.

Red and Fiona cleaned the lot. Then it was time to plant seeds.

"I wish I could help," said Ricardo, "But I have bones to dig up."

"I'll help," said Fiona, shaking her head at the dog.

Red and Fiona planted beans, carrots, pumpkins, and squash. Soon the seeds grew and made the garden beautiful. It looked like a **masterpiece**! Red asked her friends to help weed and water. Only Fiona had time to help. When it was time to pick the vegetables, only Red and Fiona did the work.

"I'll make dinner," said Red. "Each vegetable will be an **ingredient** in my **recipes** for cooking vegetable stew and pumpkin pie." Red licked her lips. "Those are **tasty** dishes."

Ricardo happened to walk by just then.

"I'd be happy to come to dinner," he said.

"You didn't help clean, weed, water, or pick. What makes you think you're invited?" asked Fiona. Red nodded firmly.

Of course, Fiona was invited, and everything was delicious.

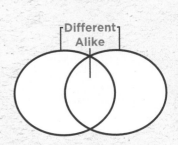

Reread for **Comprehension**

Make Inferences and Analyze
Compare and Contrast
To compare and contrast ways that people, things or events are the same and different, you need to analyze information from the story.

A Venn Diagram helps you make inferences about the characters' actions and feelings so you can compare and contrast them. Reread the story to compare and contrast Fiona with Ricardo.

Different
Alike

Comprehension

Genre

Humorous Fiction is a made-up story written to make the reader laugh.

Make Inferences and Analyze

Compare and Contrast

As you read, use your Venn Diagram.

Read to Find Out

Does this story end just like "Red and Her Friends"?

Cook-A-Doodle-Doo!

by Janet Stevens and
Susan Stevens Crummel

illustrated by Janet Stevens

Award Winning Selection

Little Red Hen's
Magnificent
Strawberry Shortcake

Peck. Peck. Peck.

"Always chicken feed! Day after day—year after year—I'm sick of it!" squawked Big Brown Rooster. "Can we get something new to eat around here? Please? Nobody's listening. What's a hungry rooster to do?"

"There's no hope. Wait a minute … " Rooster remembered a story his mama used to tell, a story handed down from chicken to chicken. The story of his famous great-grandmother, the Little Red Hen.

Rooster rushed into the chicken coop. "It has to be here," he said. He looked high and low, and there it was at last, hidden under a nest—her cookbook. *The Joy of Cooking Alone* by L. R. Hen.

Rooster carefully turned the pages. "So many **recipes**—and I thought she just baked bread! Look at the strawberry shortcake!"

"That's it! I'll make the most wonderful, **magnificent** strawberry shortcake in the whole wide world. No more chicken feed for me!"

"Yes sirree—just like Great-Granny, I'll be a cook! COOK-A-DOODLE-DO-O-O!" crowed Rooster as he pranced toward the big farmhouse.

Compare and Contrast
How is Rooster like Great-Granny? How is he different?

18

"*Cook*-a-doodle-doo?" said Dog.

"Have you lost your marbles, Rooster?" asked Cat.

"You've never cooked anything before!" said Goose.

"That doesn't matter," replied Rooster. "Cooking is in my blood—it's a family tradition. Now, who will help me?"

"Not I," said Dog.

"Not I," said Cat.

"Not I," said Goose.

And away they went.

Rooster pushed open the kitchen door. "It looks like I'm on my own … just like Great-Granny." He sighed and put on his apron.

"We'll help you."

Rooster turned, and there stood Turtle, Iguana, and Potbellied Pig.

"Do you three know anything about cooking?" Rooster asked.

"I can read recipes!" said Turtle.

"I can get stuff!" said Iguana.

"I can taste!" said Pig. "I'm an expert at tasting."

"Then we're a team," declared Rooster. "Let's get ready and start cooking!"

Turtle read the cookbook. "Heat oven to 450 degrees."

"I can do that!" said Iguana. "Look, I'll turn the knob. 150, 250, 350, 450. Hey, cooking is easy!"

Rooster put a big bowl on the table. "What's our first **ingredient**?" he asked.

"The recipe says we need flour," said Turtle.

"I can do that!" said Iguana. He dashed outside and picked a petunia. "How's this flower?"

Little Red Hen's Magnificent Strawberry Shortcake

A cookbook gives directions for making many different things to eat. Each type of food has its own recipe—a list of everything that goes into it and step-by-step directions on how to make it.

One of the oven knobs controls the temperature of the oven. The higher the number on the knob, the hotter the oven. Temperature is measured in degrees Fahrenheit (°F) or degrees Celsius (°C). On a very hot day the temperature outside can be over 100°F (38°C). Can you imagine what 450°F (232°C) feels like?

Ingredients are the different things that go into a recipe. Each ingredient may not taste good by itself, but if you put them all together in the right way, the result tastes delicious.

"No, no, no," said Rooster. "Not *that* kind of flower. We need flour for *cooking*. You know, the fluffy white stuff that's made from wheat."

"Can I taste the flour?" asked Pig.

"Not yet, Pig," said Turtle. "The recipe says to sift it first."

"What does *sift* mean?" asked Iguana.

"Hmmm," said Turtle. "I think *sift* means 'to search through' . . ."

Make sure you use a big bowl that will hold all of the ingredients. It's best to set out everything before you start cooking, so you don't have to go looking for your ingredients one-by-one like Iguana!

Flour is made from wheat grains that are finely ground. Long ago, the grinding was done by hand; now it is done by machines. Rooster's Great-Granny had to grind the grain into flour by hand, but you and Rooster can buy flour at the grocery store.

You will find many different kinds of flour at the store—including all-purpose flour, whole-wheat flour, cake flour, and high-altitude flour. Rooster's recipe calls for all-purpose flour.

Sifting adds air to the flour so it can be measured accurately. Some sifters have cranks, some have spring-action handles, and some are battery powered.

Make sure you put waxed paper on the counter before you start sifting. It will make cleanup a lot easier!

"You mean like when I sift through the garbage looking for lunch?" asked Pig.

"I can do that!" said Iguana. And he dived into the flour, throwing it everywhere!

"No, no, no," said Rooster. "Don't sift the flour like that. Put it through this sifter." Rooster turned the crank and sifted the flour into a big pile.

"Can I taste the pile?" asked Pig.

"Not yet, Pig," said Turtle. "Now we measure the flour."

"I can do that!" said Iguana. He grabbed a ruler. "The flour is four inches tall."

"No, no, no," said Rooster. "We don't want to know how *tall* it is. We want to know how *much* there is. We measure the flour with this metal measuring cup."

"We need two cups," added Turtle. "So fill it twice."

Rooster dumped the two cups of flour into the bowl.

"Can I taste it *now*?" asked Pig.

"Not yet, Pig," said Turtle. "Next we add two tablespoons of sugar, one tablespoon of baking powder, and one-half teaspoon of salt."

 Compare and Contrast
How is Pig different from Rooster?

 Measuring cups for dry ingredients are made of metal or plastic and usually come in sets of four—1 cup, 1/2 cup, 1/3 cup, and 1/4 cup. Pick the measuring cup that holds the amount you need, then dip it into the dry ingredient, getting a heaping amount. Level it off with the straight edge of a knife and let the extra fall back into the container (although Pig would be very happy if just a little fell on the floor!)

Dry ingredients can be measured in cups or grams.

1 cup = 227 grams

2 cups = 454 grams

 Some ingredients are included for flavor, but not baking powder. Even Pig thinks it tastes terrible! When baking powder is added to the shortcake, bubbles of gas form and get bigger while the cake bakes, which makes it rise.

Dry ingredients are all sifted together so they will be evenly mixed.

"I can do that!" said Iguana. He looked under the table. "But where are the tablespoons?" He looked in the teapot. "No teaspoons in here!"

"No, no, no," said Rooster. "Don't look in the teapot or under the table! These spoons are for measuring. Each holds a certain amount." Rooster measured the sugar, baking powder, and salt, poured them into the big bowl, then sifted all the dry ingredients together.

Iguana wasn't far off when he looked for tablespoons under the table and teaspoons in the teapot. Tablespoons were named after the large spoons used at the table to serve soup, and teaspoons after the smaller spoons used to stir tea.

3 teaspoons = 1 tablespoon = 14 grams

Butter is made by churning cream, the fat in cow's milk. (This doesn't mean it comes from a fat cow!) Margarine can be used instead of butter. Butter and margarine come in sticks and are easy to measure because their wrappers are marked in tablespoons.

1 stick butter = 1/2 cup = 8 tablespoons = 113 grams

Butter and margarine are two types of solid shortening, or fat, used in cooking. The name "shortcake" doesn't mean the cake is short—it refers to the shortening in the recipe.

Cool butter is "cut in" to dry ingredients by using two table knives or a pastry blender. Cut the butter into tiny pieces.

"Looks awfully white in there," said Pig. "I better taste it."

"Not yet, Pig," said Turtle. "Now we add butter. We need one stick."

"I can do that!" cried Iguana. He raced outside and broke off a branch. "How's this stick?"

"No, no, no," said Rooster. "Not *that* kind of stick. A stick of *butter*." Rooster unwrapped the butter and dropped it into the bowl.

"That butter is just sitting there like a log," said Pig. "Maybe I need to taste it."

"Not yet, Pig," said Turtle. "Next we cut in the butter."

"I can do that!" said Iguana. "Uh-oh. Scissors don't cut butter very well."

"No, no, no," said Rooster. "Don't cut the butter with scissors. Use these two table knives, like this."

Rooster cut in the butter until the mixture was crumbly.

"Looks mighty dry in there," said Pig. "Perhaps I should taste it."

"Not yet, Pig," said Turtle. "Now the recipe says to beat one egg."

"I can do that!" cried Iguana.

"No, no, no," said Rooster. "Don't beat an egg with a baseball bat! We use an eggbeater." Rooster carefully broke the egg into a dish, beat it with the eggbeater, and poured it into the big bowl.

"That looks tasty," said Pig. "Please let me taste it."

"Not yet, Pig," said Turtle. "Now add milk. We need two-thirds of a cup."

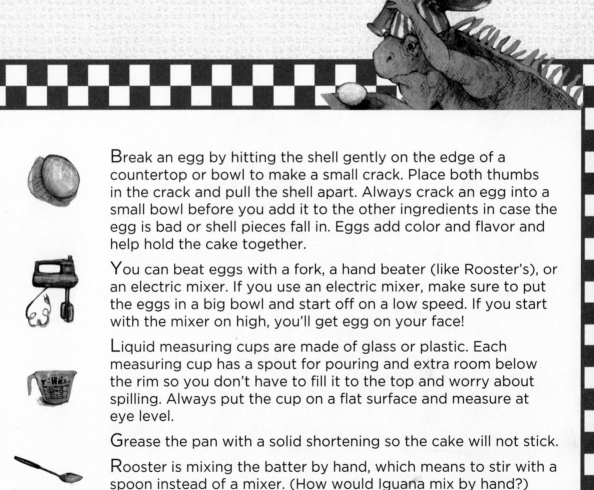

Break an egg by hitting the shell gently on the edge of a countertop or bowl to make a small crack. Place both thumbs in the crack and pull the shell apart. Always crack an egg into a small bowl before you add it to the other ingredients in case the egg is bad or shell pieces fall in. Eggs add color and flavor and help hold the cake together.

You can beat eggs with a fork, a hand beater (like Rooster's), or an electric mixer. If you use an electric mixer, make sure to put the eggs in a big bowl and start off on a low speed. If you start with the mixer on high, you'll get egg on your face!

Liquid measuring cups are made of glass or plastic. Each measuring cup has a spout for pouring and extra room below the rim so you don't have to fill it to the top and worry about spilling. Always put the cup on a flat surface and measure at eye level.

Grease the pan with a solid shortening so the cake will not stick.

Rooster is mixing the batter by hand, which means to stir with a spoon instead of a mixer. (How would Iguana mix by hand?)

"I can do that!" said Iguana. "Here, hold that glass measuring cup and I'll saw off a third. We'll use the other two-thirds to measure the milk."

"Wait," said Pig. "Why don't we fill the measuring cup to the top and I'll drink down a third?"

"No, no, no," said Rooster. "The cup has marks on it—1/3—2/3—1 cup. We'll fill it to the 2/3 mark." Rooster poured the milk into the bowl.

"It surely needs tasting now!" said Pig.

"Not yet, Pig," said Turtle. "Now we mix the dough and put it in a greased baking pan." Rooster stirred and spread as Turtle read, "Bake in the oven for fifteen to eighteen minutes."

"I can do that!" cried Iguana.

Iguana shoved the pan into the oven. "Let's see, fifteen minutes equals nine hundred seconds. I'll count them. One, two, three, four—"

"No, no, no," said Rooster, and he set the timer so that Iguana would stop counting the seconds. Pig burned his tongue on the oven door trying to taste the shortcake. Turtle studied the cookbook to see what to do next.

"Let's cut up the strawberries and whip the cream," said Turtle.

Make sure you stay nearby, so you can hear the timer when your cake is ready! Cooking times are given in hours, minutes, or seconds.
1 hour = 60 minutes
1 minute = 60 seconds

Wash the strawberries first and cut off their tops. Use a cutting board and cut each strawberry in half, then cut each half in half. (How many pieces do you have now?) Watch out for your fingers!

Whipping cream comes from cow's milk. It contains more butterfat than regular cream. Iguana might think you use a whip to whip the cream, but you could use an eggbeater or electric mixer.

When you take something out of a hot oven, make sure you use a pot holder or oven mitt.

A trick to tell if your shortcake is done: Stick a toothpick or knife in the center of the cake. If it comes out clean, without any cake sticking to it, the shortcake is ready.

Don't forget to turn off the oven when you're finished!

And they cut and cut and whipped and whipped, until
… *ding!*

Rooster grabbed the oven mitt off Iguana's head and
took the shortcake carefully out of the oven.

"Oh, it's beautiful, and it smells *sooo* good," said Pig.
"I know I have to taste it now."

"Not yet, Pig," said Turtle. "We need to let it cool."

Soon the shortcake was ready to cut. Rooster sliced
it in half.

They stacked one layer of cake, one layer of whipped cream, one layer of strawberries.

Then again—cake, cream, berries.

It looked just like the picture of the strawberry shortcake in the cookbook.

"This is the most wonderful, magnificent strawberry shortcake in the whole wide world," said Rooster. "If Great-Granny could see me now! Let's take it to the table."

"I can do that!" cried Iguana.

He yanked at the plate. The shortcake tilted …
and slid …

splat!

Right on the floor.

Pig was ready. "Now it's my turn—to taste it!"

In a split second the strawberry shortcake was
gone. Every last crumb had disappeared into the
potbelly of the pig.

"Our shortcake!" Iguana cried. "You ate it!"

"I thought it was my turn," replied Pig. "I'm the
taster, remember? And it tasted great!"

"But it was our **masterpiece**," moaned Turtle.

"And a **tasty** one, too," said Pig. "Now we can
make something else."

"Yeah …" Iguana glared. "How about a plump,
juicy roast pig?"

Pig gasped. "Roast pig? How about iguana
potpie—or—or—turtle soup!"

"No, no, no!" cried Rooster. "Listen to me! We made this shortcake as a team, and teams work together."

"But Pig ate it!" whined Turtle.

"Iguana dropped it," pouted Pig.

"Turtle should have caught it," grumbled Iguana.

"It doesn't matter," said Rooster. "The first shortcake was just for practice. It won't be as hard to make the second time!"

"Well," added Turtle, "we don't have to worry about messing up the kitchen. It's already a mess."

"So, who will help me make it again?" asked Rooster.

Pig, Turtle, and Iguana looked at each other.

"I will!" said Pig.

"I will!" said Turtle.

"I will!" said Iguana.

"Cook-a-doodle-dooooo!" crowed Rooster. "Let's get cooking again!"

Together they made the second most wonderful, magnificent strawberry shortcake in the whole wide world. And it was a lot easier than the first time!

What's Cookin' With Janet and Susan?

Janet Stevens and Susan Stevens Crummel

Authors **Janet Stevens** and **Susan Stevens Crummel** were not very close when they were growing up, but now they have as much fun working together as the animals in their story did.

They are sisters who both like animals. Janet's favorite books as a child were about animals. She still reads animal stories today. Janet likes telling old tales in new ways, just as she did in this story. The sisters wrote this book together. Then Janet created the illustrations. She's been drawing ever since she was a child.

Other books by Janet Stevens and Susan Stevens Crummel: *Jackalope* and *And the Dish Ran Away with the Spoon*

Authors' Purpose

What was the authors' purpose for writing *Cook-a-Doodle-Doo!*? Did they want to inform or entertain? How did they achieve their goal?

LOG ON Find out more about Janet Stevens and Susan Stevens Crummel at **www.macmillanmh.com**

Comprehension Check

Summarize

Summarize what happens in *Cook-a-Doodle-Doo!* Use the Venn Diagram to help you compare Pig and Rooster. Compare and contrast the main characters using descriptions of their personalities and events in the story.

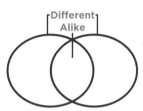

Think and Compare

1. Look at the information cards in the story. How is this extra information different from the main text? How is it similar to the main text? **Make Inferences and Analyze: Compare and Contrast**

2. What conclusion can you draw about Pig being a helpful member of the team? Use story details in your answer. **Analyze**

3. How would you apply what you have learned about these characters if you had to work on a team with Turtle, Pig, and Iguana in the future? Explain. **Apply**

4. How important is teamwork when creating a **masterpiece**? Explain your answer. **Evaluate**

5. Read "Red and Her Friends" on pages 12–13. How is it similar to *Cook-a-Doodle-Doo!*? How are the two stories different? Use details from both stories in your answer. **Reading/Writing Across Texts**

Welcome to the Bakery!

by Eric Michaels

Have you ever walked into a bakery and enjoyed the wonderful smells and tastes of freshly baked breads, pies, and cakes? Those baked goods are the results of truly hard work!

Most bakers get to work at three or four o'clock in the morning. They have to do that so the rolls, muffins, and breads will be ready to be sold before breakfast time.

When you think about all of the things sold at a bakery, the work of a baker seems amazing! Bread is just one of the things they make, and most bakeries make and sell many kinds. They bake white breads, whole wheat, rye breads, French breads, raisin breads, and pumpernickels.

How Bread Is Made

SKILL ✓ Reading a Diagram

Follow the arrows in this diagram to see how bread is made.

Bakers follow these steps to make bread.

1 Bread ingredients are mixed in a large mixer.

2 The dough rests and rises in a big mixing bowl.

7 Fresh bread is ready!

6 The loaves are baked in a big oven.

3 The dough is cut into loaf-sized pieces.

5 The loaves of dough rest and rise again.

4 The dough is kneaded, or pressed and stretched.

At the start of the day, bakers organize their work **schedule**. They plan times to bake, sell, and order supplies. They also plan the **sequence** of their baking, such as what they should bake first.

A Baker's Day

Bakers must create and mix their doughs. Every type of bread begins with a different dough. Each ingredient in the dough must be carefully weighed or measured.

Then, the **ingredients** must be mixed together. A bakery has huge mixing bowls and machines to do the mixing. After all the ingredients are mixed into a sticky dough, it must "rest" for several hours. Bread dough can't be rushed! Next, pieces of dough are cut by hand and weighed. Each piece will become one loaf of bread. But nothing is ready to be baked yet!

The dough still must be kneaded. That means that a baker must stretch it and press it over and over until it feels softer and all ingredients are completely mixed together. After kneading, the dough is shaped into loaves. Some loaves are round, some are long and thin, and others look like big braids.

It is not time to put those loaves in the oven yet! They need another "rest." Then they are finally ready to go in the oven. A bakery oven can be as big as a room. The baker watches carefully as the breads bake. When they are crusty and golden brown, the loaves are taken out of the oven to cool. Then they are ready to be sold.

Running a Bakery

A bakery is a business, so a good baker must also be a good business person. Buying ingredients, setting prices, and figuring out **profits**, or how much money is made, are all part of the bakery business.

Running a bakery is hard work, but baking beautiful, delicious things can be fun and rewarding. After all, people are always happy to enjoy the tasty treats that bakers create!

Connect and Compare

1. Look at the text and diagram on page 41. What happens before bread dough is cut into loaves? What happens after the baker kneads the dough? **Reading a Diagram**

2. What kind of a person do you think would make a good baker? Why do you think that? **Analyze**

3. Think about this article and *Cook-A-Doodle-Doo!* What tips could a real baker give the animals? **Reading/Writing Across Texts**

Social Studies Activity

Research baking recipes from other countries. Draw and label a diagram showing how to make the tastiest recipe you find. Give the diagram a title.

 Find out more about baking at **www.macmillanmh.com**

Writer's Craft

Vary Sentences

Vary the length of your sentences to help your writing flow better. Too many short sentences make your writing choppy. Too many long sentences may make your writing tiring to read.

Write About Something You Like to Do

I wrote a topic sentence first. Then I briefly described all the steps in order.

Here I joined two short, related sentences to make a compound sentence.

Making Blueberry Pancakes

by Marcus G.

My favorite thing to do is make blueberry pancakes. I am really good at making them big, blue, and round. First, I have to mix water into the pancake mix. Next, I put all of the blueberries in a bowl and mash them with a fork. Then, I mix the berries into the batter. It's fun to watch the batter turn blue. Finally, I pour the batter into the pan in perfect circles, and my dad cooks them. Of course, the best thing about blueberry pancakes is eating them!

Your Turn

Write a paragraph that explains something you like to do. It may be about a sport, a hobby, or anything else. Start with a topic sentence. Then explain the activity step-by-step. Along the way, be sure to explain why you like this activity. Use the Writer's Checklist to check your writing.

Writer's Checklist

✓ **Ideas and Content:** Is my explanation clear?

✓ **Organization:** Did I write a topic sentence? Did I use words like *first, next, then,* and *finally* to show the order of steps?

✓ **Voice:** Do I show that I like this activity?

✓ **Word Choice:** Did I use descriptive words?

☐ **Sentence Fluency:** Did I **vary** sentence lengths?

✓ **Conventions:** If I used the verbs *be, do,* and *have,* did I use the correct forms? Did I check my spelling?

Getting Along

Talk About It

People can have different ideas and still work together. What do you do when someone disagrees with you?

LOG ON Find out more about getting along at **www.macmillanmh.com**

Vocabulary

beamed	fabric
argued	purchased
possessions	quarreling

Dictionary

Multiple-Meaning Words are words that have more than one meaning.

Use a dictionary to find two meanings of the word *beamed*.

Community Works

by Jenna Rabin

One bright day, as the sunlight **beamed** through the windows, Mr. Turner's class started to plan the third-grade community service project.

"OK," said Mr. Turner. "Let's share some ideas and listen to each other."

A few students raised their hands. Mr. Turner called on Mark. "We could clean up the small park—pick up trash and paint the benches," said Mark.

Rachel got annoyed. She **argued** with Mark. "You just want that park clean for yourself. Everyone else uses the big park across town. I think we should serve meals at the homeless shelter."

"Now, Rachel. Everyone should have a chance to share his or her ideas. It's okay to disagree, but we should still treat each other nicely."

"Sorry, Mr. Turner," Rachel said.

Jen cut in, "There are people who don't have many **possessions**, not even warm clothing. We could collect **fabric** for making nice, warm clothes for them!"

Cara added, "I read about a class that raised money and **purchased** notebooks and pencils for kids from a discount store."

"We could do crafts with people in nursing homes or hospitals," said Maria.

"Crafts?" groaned Sameer. "I'm really bad at crafts. I'm all thumbs! But how about a walk-a-thon. I'm a fast walker, and we'd get exercise," he said. This made everyone laugh and stop their **quarreling** over who had the best idea.

Then Mr. Turner spoke. "All of your ideas are great. I'm going to write them on the board. Then we will take a class vote. This way we can choose a community service project that most people want to do."

The students agreed this was a good plan.

Reread for **Comprehension**

Make Inferences and Analyze
Draw Conclusions

Authors don't tell you every detail in a story. You have to analyze clues the author does give and what you already know to draw conclusions.

Reread the story to draw conclusions about how one character feels about their community service suggestion. A Conclusion Map can help you draw conclusions based on the inferences you have made.

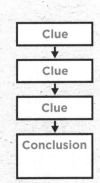

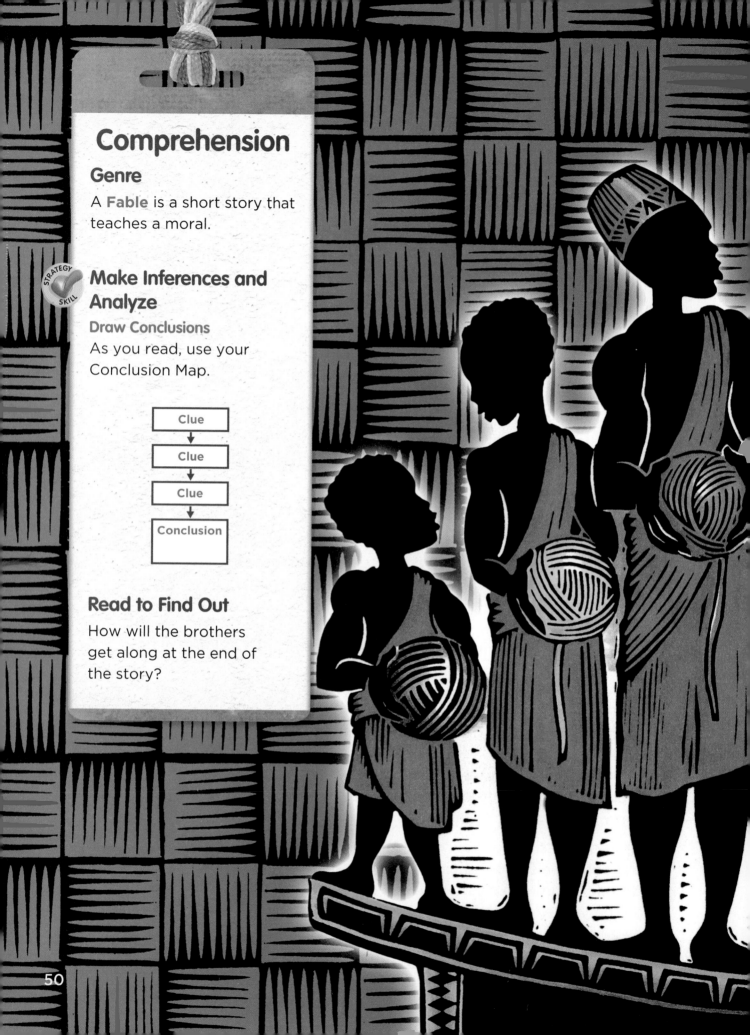

Comprehension

Genre

A **Fable** is a short story that teaches a moral.

Make Inferences and Analyze

Draw Conclusions
As you read, use your Conclusion Map.

Clue
↓
Clue
↓
Clue
↓
Conclusion

Read to Find Out

How will the brothers get along at the end of the story?

Seven Spools of Thread

A KWANZAA STORY

BY ANGELA SHELF MEDEARIS

ILLUSTRATED BY DANIEL MINTER

Award Winning Selection

51

In a small African village in the country of Ghana there lived an old man and his seven sons. After the death of his wife, the old man became both father and mother to the boys. The seven brothers were handsome young men. Their skin was as smooth and dark as the finest mahogany wood. Their limbs were as straight and strong as warriors' spears.

But they were a disappointment to their father. From morning until night, the family's small home was filled with the sound of the brothers' **quarreling**.

As soon as the sun brought forth a new day, the brothers began to argue. They **argued** all morning about how to tend the crops. They argued all afternoon about the weather.

"It is hot," said the middle son.

"No—a cool breeze is blowing!" said the second son.

They argued all evening about when to return home.

"It will be dark soon," the youngest said. "Let's finish this row and begin anew tomorrow."

"No, it's too early to stop," called the third son.

"Can't you see the sun is setting?" shouted the sixth son.

And so it would continue until the moon **beamed** down and the stars twinkled in the sky.

At mealtime, the young men argued until the stew was cold and the fu fu was hard.

"You gave him more than you gave me," whined the third son.

"I divided the food equally," said their father.

"I will starve with only this small portion on my plate," complained the youngest.

"If you don't want it, I'll eat it!" said the oldest son. He grabbed a handful of meat from his brother's plate.

"Stop being so greedy!" said the youngest.

And so it went on every night. It was often morning before the seven brothers finished dinner.

One sad day, the old man died and was buried. At sunrise the next morning, the village Chief called the brothers before him.

"Your father has left an inheritance," said the Chief.

The brothers whispered excitedly among themselves.

"I know my father left me everything because I am the oldest son," said the oldest.

"I know my father left me everything because I am the youngest son," said the youngest.

"He left everything to me," said the middle son. "I know I was his favorite."

"Eeeh!" said the second son. "Everything is mine!"

The brothers began shouting and shoving. Soon, all seven were rolling around on the ground, hitting and kicking each other.

"Stop that this instant!" the Chief shouted.

The brothers stopped fighting. They shook the dust off their clothes and sat before the Chief, eyeing each other suspiciously.

"Your father has decreed that all of his property and **possessions** will be divided among you equally," said the Chief. "But first, by the time the moon rises tonight, you must learn how to make gold out of these spools of silk thread. If you do not, you will be turned out of your home as beggars."

The oldest brother received blue thread. The next brother, red. The next, yellow. The middle son was given orange thread; the next, green; the next, black; and the youngest son received white thread. For once, the brothers were speechless.

The Chief spoke again. "From this moment forward, you must not argue among yourselves or raise your hands in anger towards one another. If you do, your father's property and all his possessions will be divided equally among the poorest of the villagers. Go quickly; you only have a little time."

The brothers bowed to the Chief and hurried away.

Draw Conclusions
Why were the brothers speechless after listening to the Chief?

When the seven Ashanti brothers arrived at their farm, something unusual happened. They sat side by side, from the oldest to the youngest, without saying anything unkind to each other.

"My brothers," the oldest said after a while, "let us shake hands and make peace among ourselves."

"Let us never argue or fight again," said the youngest brother.

The brothers placed their hands together and held each other tightly.

For the first time in years, peace rested within the walls of their home.

"My brothers," said the third son quietly, "surely our father would not turn us into the world as beggars."

"I agree," said the middle son. "I do not believe our father would have given us the task of turning thread into gold if it were impossible."

"Could it be," said the oldest son, "that there might be small pieces of gold in this thread?"

The sun beamed hotly overhead. Yellow streams of light crept inside the hut. Each brother held up his spool of thread. The beautiful colors sparkled in the sunlight. But there were no nuggets of gold in these spools.

"I'm afraid not, my brother," said the sixth son. "But that was a good idea."

"Thank you, my brother," said the oldest.

"Could it be," said the youngest, "that by making something from this thread we could earn a fortune in gold?"

"Perhaps," said the oldest, "we could make cloth out of this thread and sell it. I believe we can do it."

"This is a good plan," said the middle son. "But we do not have enough of any one color to make a full bolt of cloth."

"What if," said the third son, "we weave the thread together to make a cloth of many colors?"

"But our people do not wear cloth like that," said the fifth son. "We wear only cloth of one color."

"Maybe," said the second, "we could make a cloth that is so special, everyone will want to wear it."

"My brothers," said the sixth son, "we could finish faster if we all worked together."

"I know we can succeed," said the middle son.

The seven Ashanti brothers went to work. Together they cut the wood to make a loom. The younger brothers held the pieces together while the older brothers assembled the loom.

They took turns weaving cloth out of their spools of
thread. They made a pattern of stripes and shapes that
looked like the wings of birds. They used all the colors—
blue, red, yellow, orange, green, black, and white. Soon the
brothers had several pieces of beautiful multicolored cloth.

When the cloth was finished, the seven brothers took turns neatly folding the brightly colored **fabric**. Then they placed it into seven baskets and put the baskets on their heads.

The brothers formed a line from the oldest to the youngest and began the journey to the village. The sun slowly made a golden path across the sky. The brothers hurried down the long, dusty road as quickly as they could.

As soon as they entered the marketplace, the seven Ashanti brothers called out, "Come and buy the most wonderful cloth in the world! Come and buy the most wonderful cloth in the world!"

They unfolded a bolt and held it up for all to see. The multicolored fabric glistened like a rainbow. A crowd gathered around the seven Ashanti brothers.

"Oh," said one villager. "I have never seen cloth so beautiful! Look at the unusual pattern!"

"Ah," said another. "This is the finest fabric in all the land! Feel the texture!"

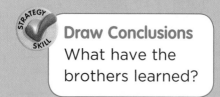

Draw Conclusions
What have the brothers learned?

The brothers smiled proudly. Suddenly, a man dressed in magnificent robes pushed his way to the front of the crowd. Everyone stepped back respectfully. It was the King's treasurer. He rubbed the cloth between the palms of his hands. Then he held it up to the sunlight.

"What a thing of beauty," he said, fingering the material. "This cloth will make a wonderful gift for the King! I must have all of it."

The seven brothers whispered together.

"Cloth fit for a king," said the oldest, "should be **purchased** at a price only a king can pay. It is yours for one bag of gold."

"Sold," said the King's treasurer. He untied his bag of gold and spilled out many pieces for the brothers.

The seven Ashanti brothers ran out of the marketplace and back down the road to their village.

From that day until this, the seven Ashanti brothers have worked together, farming the land.

And they have worked peacefully, in honor of their father.

Sticks in a bundle are unbreakable.
—*African Proverb*

WEAVING A TALE WITH ANGELA AND DANIEL

Author **Angela Shelf Medearis** wrote this story to celebrate the African American holiday Kwanzaa. When Angela was growing up, there were no books for her to read about her African American heritage. Today she writes books about African Americans so readers can feel proud of who they are.

Illustrator **Daniel Minter** often carves and paints on wood, just as he did for this story. Woodcarving is an important part of traditional African art. Daniel's carvings help keep these traditional arts alive.

Other books by Angela Shelf Medearis: *Too Much Talk* and *The Freedom Riddle*

 LOG ON Find out more about Angela Shelf Medearis and Daniel Minter at **www.macmillanmh.com**

Author's Purpose

Did Angela Shelf Medearis write this story to explain, inform, or entertain? What clues show readers her purpose for writing?

72

Comprehension Check

Summarize

Summarize the plot of *Seven Spools of Thread.* Use your Conclusion Map to help you recall clues that tell how the brothers behave at the end.

Clue
↓
Clue
↓
Clue
↓
Conclusion

Think and Compare

1. Instead of ordering them to stop **quarreling**, the Chief ordered the brothers to make gold from thread. Why do you think he did that? Use your Conclusion Map to help you answer. **Make Inferences and Analyze: Draw Conclusions**

2. Look back at page 61. What lesson about teamwork are the brothers beginning to learn? Use story details in your answer. **Analyze**

3. Think about a quarrel you had. What positive lesson did you learn? **Apply**

4. The brothers taught the villagers how to weave the special cloth. Why is that better than giving the villagers their money? Explain. **Evaluate**

5. Read "Community Works" on pages 48–49. How is the problem in this story similar to the problem in *Seven Spools of Thread*? How are the solutions to the problems different? Use details from both stories in your answer. **Reading/Writing Across Texts**

Our Class Newsletter

by Mrs. Simon's Third-Grade Class

On Monday Mrs. Simon helped us settle an argument between Marcus and Nathan. We have been learning about **conflict** resolution in her class. A conflict is a problem between people. To **resolve** something means to solve it. So conflict resolution is solving problems so we can get along better.

Here's what happened: Marcus couldn't find his homework. He thought that Nathan took it. Marcus was really mad.

First, Mrs. Simon told Marcus to cool off. Next, she asked him to calmly explain what was bothering him. Marcus said, "I'm mad at Nathan because I think he took my homework."

Mrs. Simon asked Nathan to understand how Marcus felt. Nathan said, "I'd be mad, too, if someone took my homework. That's why I would never do that."

The class made a list of possible solutions and discussed them. We thought it would be best for Nathan to help Marcus look for his homework. Guess what happened? When Nathan helped, Marcus found his paper. It was in his notebook all along. We learned that conflict resolution works!

Our Classroom Rules

Reading Rules

In our class we **respect** each other. These rules can help us stop problems before they start!

- Be polite to each other.
- Keep your hands to yourself.
- Raise your hand to speak.
- Follow the teacher's directions.

Connect and Compare

1. Look at the classroom rules. Why do you think the second rule is important? **Reading Rules**

2. How can Mrs. Simon's tips help you in your own life? When might you need to use them? **Apply**

3. Think about *Seven Spools of Thread*. Which steps did the brothers use to solve their problem? How were their steps similar to Nathan's? **Reading/Writing Across Texts**

Social Studies Activity

Write a list of rules for your school playground. Compare lists with a partner. Then combine your lists. Share your final list of rules with the class.

 Find out more about getting along at **www.macmillanmh.com**

Writer's Craft

Precise Words

Sometimes **precise words** that show details are included to make writing smoother and clearer. This is especially important when writing instructions.

I used precise words to tell how to make a paper place mat.

I added some details to make my sentences smoother and clearer.

Make a Rainbow Place Mat

by Peter K.

A rainbow-colored place mat is easy to make. You will need tape, scissors, and paper in several colors.

1. Fold a piece of paper in half.
2. Starting from the fold, make five cuts that end one inch from the paper's edge. Unfold.
3. Cut one-inch-wide strips from the other pieces of paper.
4. Weave the strips between the cuts you made. Then, tape the strips together.
5. Your place mat is ready to use!

Your Turn

Write a poster with directions for making something to use, eat, or wear. Be sure to add precise words that provide details and make sentences read clearly and flow smoothly. Use the Writer's Checklist to check your writing.

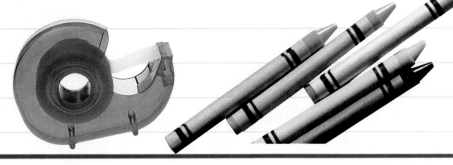

Writer's Checklist

☑ **Ideas and Content:** Did I give enough information to make this project?

☑ **Organization:** Are the directions in order?

☑ **Voice:** Did I write directly to my readers?

☐ **Word Choice:** Did I choose **precise words** that make my meaning clear?

☑ **Sentence Fluency:** Did I add words to provide details and make sentences flow smoothly?

☑ **Conventions:** Did I use linking verbs correctly? Did I use the correct punctuation at the end of complete sentences?

Talk About It

Why do people need the natural resources shown on these pages?

LOG ON Find out more about natural resources at **www.macmillanmh.com**

Protecting Our Natural Resources

WASHINGTON WEED WHACKERS

WHAT ALIEN SPECIES IS CREEPING ALONG THE SHORES OF PUGET SOUND?

Comprehension

Genre

Nonfiction Articles give information about real people, places, or things.

Monitor Comprehension

Compare and Contrast
When you look for similarities, you compare two or more things or ideas. When you look for differences, you contrast them.

The "weed whackers" of Lincoln Elementary, in Mount Vernon, Washington

Spartina is a perfectly good plant. It creates a habitat and food for many fish and wildlife. So why do the kids at Lincoln Elementary School in Mount Vernon, Washington, want to get rid of it? It's because spartina **shouldn't** live on the West Coast. In Washington State's Puget Sound, spartina has turned into a life-choking weed.

Spartina is **native** to the East Coast. There, native plants and animals keep it from growing out of control. Besides providing a wetland habitat, spartina's roots stop soil from being washed away in the tide. However, in Washington these traits are not helpful. Spartina is an alien species because it does not grow there naturally.

AN ALIEN ATTACKS!

Since no animals eat spartina in Puget Sound, it grows in thick **clumps**, crowding out native plants. Its roots hurt rather than help. "It clogs up all the mud and changes the shape of the mud flats," explains student Seth Morris. In the East it creates a good habitat, but in the West, it has caused crabs, snails, salmon, and shorebirds to leave because there is less food.

This photo shows how spartina is spreading in Puget Sound and has crowded out native plants.

When the kids at Lincoln Elementary School took on the spartina problem, they didn't know how the plant got to the Northwest. The kids contacted local experts and hit the books to do some **research**.

WHERE DID IT COME FROM?

Students Seth Morris and Anna Hansen reported that spartina came to Puget Sound in a few ways. "Spartina goes back to the late 1800s, when it came here from the East Coast," Seth explains. Settlers wanted to raise oysters in the West. They packed them in wet spartina to keep them fresh. When the oysters were put in new beds in Puget Sound, it made spartina seeds **sprout**.

Spartina was also introduced when duck hunters planted it to attract more ducks. Engineers brought the plant in to keep soil from washing away, and farmers planted it to feed their cattle.

TAKING ACTION

The classes worked in teams. One team researched Padilla Bay. Another team made drawings of spartina and its effects on the shore. The third team worked to get the word out about spartina. All the kids wrote letters to state lawmakers, urging them to help.

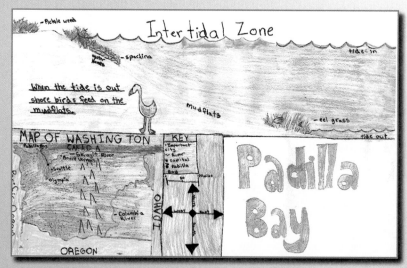

A student's drawing shows where spartina has invaded Padilla Bay.

Getting rid of spartina takes lots of hard work and money. That's why the students wanted to teach the community about the weed. First, they held town meetings to discuss spartina's impact on the environment. They also traveled to the state capitol in Olympia to talk about the problem. The kids even headed to Padilla Bay to snip off spartina seed heads to keep the weed from spreading.

"One of the big lessons we learned from this project," says their teacher, Teresa Vaughn, "was that we can't take care of the problem by just taking care of it in our bay. This is a problem for the entire Northwest coast."

The kids know that saving Padilla Bay will be hard work. It took decades for the spartina problem to take root. It'll take many years to get rid of it.

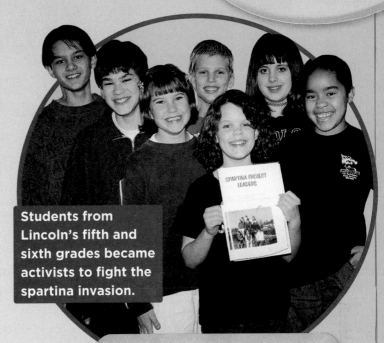

Students from Lincoln's fifth and sixth grades became activists to fight the spartina invasion.

Think and Compare

STRATEGY SKILL

1. What is the difference between spartina growth in the East and in Washington?

2. Why is spartina described as an alien?

3. What do you think is the hardest part of what the kids at Lincoln Elementary School did? Explain.

4. How have people brought on the problems described in "Saving Egypt's Great Desert" and "Washington Weed Whackers"?

Up a Creek

Test Strategy

Think and Search

The answer is in more than one place. Keep reading to find the answer.

Steelhead trout

Students work hard to keep sediment from clogging up the creek.

Students in Jean Mahoney's class worked all year to clean up Arana Creek. The creek winds around Santa Cruz, California. It is part of the Arana Gulch watershed. A watershed is an area where water from rivers, creeks, rain, or snow drains into a larger body of water.

Watersheds are ideal habitats for steelhead trout to lay eggs, but the Arana Gulch area is polluted. The creek is clogged with sediment, or loose dirt, that falls into the bay and smothers fish eggs.

After Mahoney's class learned about the area's plants and animals, they went to work. They picked up trash and removed weeds. Then they planted trees and grasses to help hold the soil together. That way the creek doesn't fill with sediment.

After they helped control soil erosion, the students looked for a way to help the steelhead make it safely to the bay. They changed how the water flowed, making it easier for the fish to get through.

The following spring they tested the water temperature and sediment levels. Conditions were just right for the trout!

Go On ▶

Directions: Answer the questions.

1. **How does pollution affect fish in a natural habitat?**

   A   It creates a watershed to protect them.
   B   It makes it hard for fish to swim and for their eggs to hatch.
   C   It decreases the average water temperature.
   D   It reduces the amount of sediment, making it easier to swim.

2. **How would you describe the students in Ms. Mahoney's class?**

   A   excited about trout fishing
   B   unhappy about working outside the classroom
   C   interested in protecting the environment
   D   tired of picking up trash and weeds

3. **What is the BEST way to protect steelhead trout eggs?**

   A   Prevent soil erosion.
   B   Create man-made lakes.
   C   Forbid fishing in the bay.
   D   Drain the rivers and creeks.

4. **In what ways was Arana Creek better off after Jean Mahoney's class worked on it?**

5. **Many students volunteer their time to help fight pollution and improve the environment. Would you be willing to give up your time? Why or why not?**

Tip
Keep reading. The answer may be in more than one place.

Write to a Prompt

"Washington Weed Whackers" is about kids working to solve the spartina problem. Imagine you are one of those kids. You are chosen to appear on TV to talk about the problem. While you are on TV, something unexpected happens. Write a story about it.

The beginning of my story explains the setting, or where the story takes place.

A Very Big Surprise

Today was the big day! I had volunteered to talk about spartina on TV. I walked into the studio ready for my big TV break.

Soon, we went on live. First I answered questions. Then I said, "We need to educate people about the spartina problem, but that takes lots of time and money."

Then the host said, "We have someone here who can help you with that."

Suddenly, the President of the United States walked onto the stage. "I think I can help," he said. The President handed me a check for two million dollars! "Do you think this will help your class tackle the spartina problem?" I just stood there nodding!

"I guess she's speechless," the host said.

Writing Prompt

Imagine that you and your class are trying to solve a problem in your community. It is the first day of the project and something unusual happens. Write a story about your unusual day. Make sure your story has a beginning, a middle, and an ending.

Writer's Checklist

- ☑ Ask yourself, who will read my story?
- ☑ Plan your writing before beginning.
- ☑ Use details to support your story.
- ☑ Be sure your story has a plot (beginning, middle, and ending), characters, and setting.
- ☑ Use your best spelling, grammar, and punctuation.

Getting Involved

Talk About It

What are some ways that you can get involved to help your family or community?

LOG ON Find out more about getting involved at **www.macmillanmh.com**

Vocabulary

tour	slogan
volunteers	grownups
community	deserve
thrilled	interviewed

STRATEGY SKILL

Context Clues

Examples can help you figure out the meaning of unknown words.

Use the example in the story to figure out the meaning of *slogan*.

GORILLA GARDEN

by Michael Feldman

Have you ever taken a **tour** of a zoo? If so, it's likely that the person who led you through the zoo helped you to learn a lot about the animals.

Amelia Rinas is a high school student who lives in Ohio. One day Amelia visited the Cleveland Metroparks Zoo. She worried about the gorillas she saw there. She wondered if they were getting the right foods.

Amelia read all she could about gorillas and learned what they like to eat. Then she started a "gorilla garden." She grows the fruits and vegetables that gorillas love to eat. Some of those foods are tomatoes, carrots, and strawberries. Amelia works with other **volunteers** in her **community** who use their extra time to help Amelia and the gorillas. When they take the food to the zoo, the gorillas are **thrilled**. They look so excited!

Who is responsible for Amelia's interest in animals? Amelia is a member of Roots & Shoots. Its members are young people who care about animals and the environment. They helped Amelia understand that animals need our care, too. The **slogan** on the Roots & Shoots Web site is "Inspire, take action, make a difference." These words tell what the group is all about. The group urges kids and **grownups**, including parents and teachers, to do what they can to make a difference where they live.

Amelia believes that both people and animals **deserve** to be treated well.

When **interviewed** about her project, Amelia said, "I joined Roots & Shoots because I wanted to make a difference in the world."

There are many ways to make a difference in the world. Amelia Rinas's gorilla garden has helped make gorillas happier and healthier.

Reread for Comprehension

STRATEGY SKILL

Monitor Comprehension
Author's Purpose

As you read, it is important to monitor your comprehension, or check your understanding. To monitor your understanding of an article, think about the author's purpose. An author writes to entertain, inform, or persuade.

Using an Author's Purpose Chart helps you figure out why an author wrote an article. Reread the article to find clues to the author's purpose.

Clues

↓

Author's Purpose

Comprehension

Genre

Nonfiction Articles give information about real people, places, or things.

Monitor Comprehension

Author's Purpose

As you read, use your Author's Purpose Map.

Clues

↓

Author's Purpose

Read to Find Out

What does the author want you to know about Angel?

94

Here's My Dollar

By Gary Soto

Award Winning Author

Angel poses with her cat.

How tall is a hero? If you had ever met nine-year-old Angel Arellano, you'd know a hero is four feet two inches tall. Angel's story began on Thanksgiving Day. She was in the kitchen listening to her Great-Grandmother Sandy.

"The zoo has money problems," Great-Grandmother Sandy remarked.

Angel listened. She heard that Fresno's Chaffee Zoo didn't have enough money to take care of its animals. Angel wondered what would happen to the elephants, the hippo, and her favorite reptile, the boa constrictor.

Angel loved animals. She planned to study them and become a zoologist when she grew up. In their own apartment in Fresno, Angel's family had four cats—Buster, Krystal, Rex, and Oreo. Angel took good care of them and made sure that they always had food and water.

Author's Purpose
Why does the author tell us about Angel's pets?

Angel holds a skink at the Chaffee Zoo.

Angel felt sorry for the zoo animals. While the **grownups** were cooking Thanksgiving dinner, Angel was cooking up a way to help the animals. She decided to write a letter to show how she felt.

When she finished writing, Angel showed the letter to her mom and her aunt. They changed some of the words and fixed the spelling. Then Angel copied her letter onto fancy stationery and added a **slogan** at the bottom: "Give a dollar, save a life." She slipped a dollar into the envelope and addressed it to *The Fresno Bee*, the local newspaper.

Angel's letter to *The Fresno Bee*

Dear Fresno bee,

Thanksgiving day

My name is angel and I am nine. I heard that the Chaffee zoo is having money problems. I am very worried for the animals. I am worried because they might not have enough food or water or even might not have a home. They deserve to have a home and be safe and warm. I think that if every body in Fresno gave $1.00 to the Chaffee zoo it would help alot. Here's my dollar.

Angelica
Arellano
age 9
Fresno

Give a dollar save a life

Angel hoped that other people might send a dollar, too, after they had read her letter. She didn't know that the zoo needed three million dollars, but that wouldn't have stopped her anyhow. Angel was a girl on a mission!

A week later, a man from *The Fresno Bee* came to take a picture of Angel. A few days after that, Angel's letter was published in *The Fresno Bee*. Almost immediately, people began sending in checks and dollar bills. Angel's letter was working!

Child's Call to Aid the Zoo

Angel Arellano collects money for the Chaffee Zoo.

By Jim Davis

Nine-year-old Angel Arellano is sparking a grass-roots effort to help the Chaffee Zoo through its financial plight. The little girl sent a letter to *The Bee* and enclosed a $1 donation for the zoo. She asked others to donate as well. "I just hope it will help, " Angel said. "I want the animals to be safe and warm and let them get fed like my letter said." Dozens have followed Angel's lead, sending donations ranging from $1 to a $1,000 check that arrived Thursday. After just two days' mail, the zoo has received $5,084.

Text from an article about Angel in
The Fresno Bee, December 6, 2003

Hippos love the zoo's shallow river.

At school, Angel went to each classroom to read the letter that appeared in the newspaper. She asked her schoolmates to give money to the zoo. An empty water jug was placed in each classroom and in the main office. Students—and parents—began to fill the jugs with coins and dollar bills.

Angel's letter had touched the **community** of Fresno—and beyond. Donations for the Chaffee Zoo began to arrive from all over California. One donation came from as far away as England. It seemed as if the whole world wanted to help the zoo.

THE CHAFFEE

Angel feeds an apple to Angolia, the giraffe.

The people at the Chaffee Zoo were **thrilled**. They invited Angel and her family to the zoo. They wanted to thank Angel in person and give her a private **tour**.

At the zoo, Angel fed grapes to the chimpanzees. She fed the hippo and the buffalo, too. In a daring mood, Angel placed a slice of apple in her mouth. She stretched her neck toward Angolia, the giraffe, who leaned its long neck down and swiped the apple from her mouth!

Angel went on being a regular kid—for a while. Before long, she was asked to make public appearances to talk about the zoo. The zoo still needed money, and Angel was happy to help. The principal of her school drove her to other schools in the area. He was just as concerned about the zoo animals as Angel.

"The zoo needs your help," Angel told the other children. "We can all make a difference."

During these appearances, Angel autographed pieces of paper, posters, and lots of shirts and caps. When reporters **interviewed** her, she tried to be herself. She spoke from her heart.

Angel prepares to make a public service announcement.

Next, Angel was asked to appear on television. She was invited to be on a popular talk show. Angel flew from Fresno to Los Angeles. It was the first time she was ever on a plane!

At the television studio, Angel entered the stage to applause and her favorite rock music. She smiled and waved. The audience was rooting for her. They were rooting for the zoo animals back in Fresno, too.

More donations arrived after Angel's appearance on television. The Chaffee Zoo got larger and larger checks. One was for $10,000. Another was for $15,000. And one was for $50,000!

Of course, many donations were still just for one dollar. Children were sending in what they had, just as Angel had done on Thanksgiving Day.

Angel boards a plane to make a television appearance.

Zookeeper Mary helps Angel hold a boa constrictor.

Everyone was behind Angel and the zoo. High school teams held car washes to raise money. **Volunteers** showed up at the zoo to help paint and clean up. A local business made T-shirts with a picture of the zoo on the front.

The zookeepers were very happy. Ray Navarro is the person most responsible for the animals. He has hauled thousands of buckets of water for the animals. He has pushed wheelbarrows of hay for the elephants, the giraffes, and the zebras. "Angel opened the eyes of Fresno," said Ray. "She made us see that people can make a difference."

Author's Purpose
Why did the author choose to write about Angel?

The campaign started with a single dollar from Angel. In six months, the Chaffee Zoo received more than $600,000. The zoo has used some of the money to fix the pathway to the reptile house where the boa constrictor lives. It has also put in cushioned floors in the giraffe barn, plastered the seal pool, and fixed the rain forest bridge. Buildings have been painted and repaired, too.

The campaign to save the Chaffee Zoo has been exciting. People from Fresno are proud that a young girl woke up their own community spirit. The zoo is looking better and better. And even though the zoo animals can't speak human languages, if they could, they might say, "You are a hero to us, Angel Arellano. You **deserve** our thanks for saving our zoo."

The zoo's seals enjoy a swim in a newly plastered pool, thanks to Angel.

Here's Our Author

Gary Soto was born and raised in Fresno, California, which is also the hometown of the Chaffee Zoo. He has written many poems and stories for children and adults. In his spare time, Gary loves to read, play tennis and basketball, and travel. He still visits Fresno often, and there is a library named for him at Winchell Elementary School in Fresno.

Other books by Gary Soto: *Baseball in April* and *Chato's Kitchen*

LOG ON Find out more about Gary Soto at **www.macmillanmh.com**

Author's Purpose

Suppose you were the author of *Here's My Dollar*. Describe why you wrote this article and how you achieved your goal. Did you want to inform readers about Angel Arellano, persuade readers to do something, or both?

Comprehension Check

Summarize

Summarize "Here's My Dollar." Use your Author's Purpose Chart to help you.

Clues

↓

Author's Purpose

Think and Compare

1. Why do you think Gary Soto wrote "Here's My Dollar"? **Monitor Comprehension: Author's Purpose**

2. Reread page 98. Why do you think *The Fresno Bee* published Angel's letter and her photo? **Analyze**

3. Think of a good cause in your own community, such as a school, library, or park, that needs help. How would you encourage people to help? **Apply**

4. What would happen if someone used a similar fund-raising idea and **slogan** to help another zoo in another part of the world? Use information from the story to support your ideas. **Synthesize**

5. Reread "Gorilla Garden" on pages 92–93. How are Amelia and Angel alike? Describe the different ways they help animals. **Reading/Writing Across Texts**

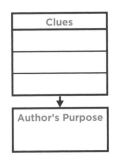

Neighbors

Poetry

Poetry uses rhyme, rhythm, and repetition to express feelings and ideas.

SKILL

Literary Elements

A **Rhyme Scheme** is the pattern of rhymes in the last words of lines.

Repetition happens when words or phrases are repeated throughout a poem. A line that is repeated throughout is called a **refrain**.

The last line of each stanza is the refrain.

When I had the sniffles,
Your mom sent me stew.
You needed a project.
My daddy helped you.
Your dad helps us paint from ceiling to floor.
Neighbors are friends that live just next door.

I call you up
When I know you feel down.
When Fluffy was lost,
We looked all over town.
It's my turn to rake when your arms get too sore.
Neighbors are friends that live just next door.

—Mari Paz Pradillo

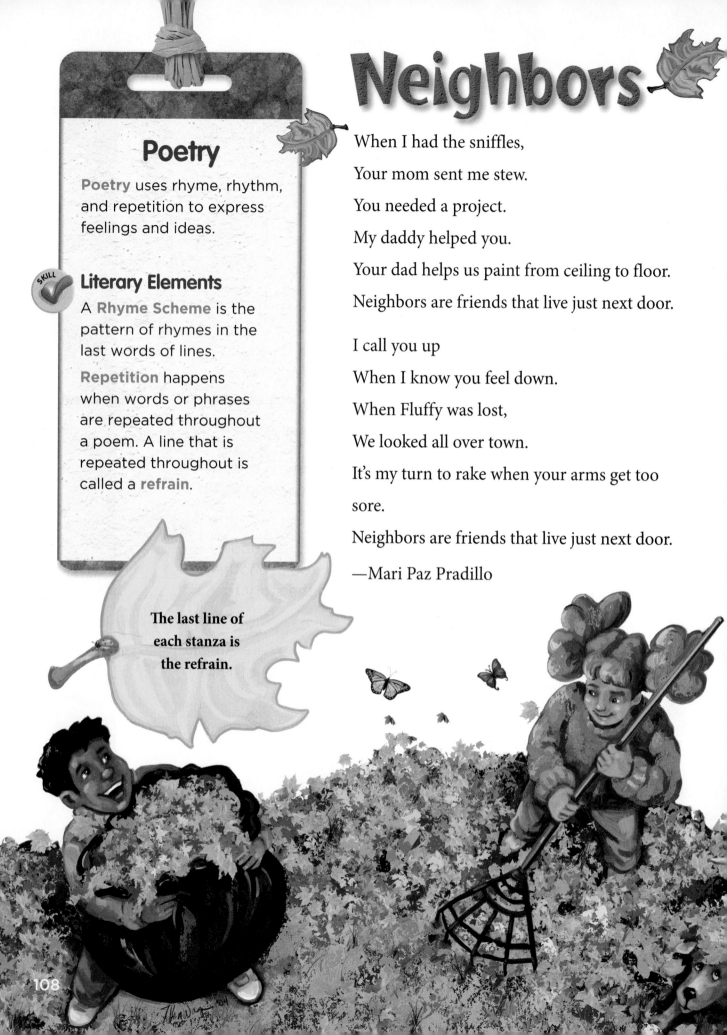

Recycling

Tucker Connors collected the papers
And Maya Ling tied them with string
Maya helped Tucker carry the papers
All the way to the recycling bins

Won Tan collected the cans
And Ruby Dean washed them all clean
Ruby helped Won carry the cans
All the way to the recycling bins

When we recycle, we help the plants
We help the creatures, from eagles to ants
We help make the world a healthier place
For one and for all in the human race

—J. Z. Belle

Plants and *ants* rhyme, as do *place* and *race*. The rhyme scheme for this stanza is AA BB.

Connect and Compare

SKILL

1. What are some other repetitions in "Recycling"? **Repetition**

2. What do you think the poet wants you to know about neighbors? **Analyze**

3. Compare these two poems about helping and *Here's My Dollar*. What is the common theme among these selections? How are they different? **Reading/Writing Across Texts**

LOG ON Find out more about poetry at **www.macmillanmh.com**

109

Write a Personal Essay

Writer's Craft

A Strong Opening
Good writers include a **strong opening** to get their readers involved. They may use an interesting question, quotation, or description.

My opening question gets readers involved.

I wrote directly to kids who care about skateboarding.

No Place to Skateboard

by Carol L.

Why don't the kids in my town have a skateboard park? I think it is a big problem. Dad said I should write to our mayor. I wrote and told him why a skateboard park would be safer for kids and better for everyone. Yesterday he wrote back and said that my idea was good. Now the town is going to build a special park for skateboarding. If you want a place to skateboard, write a letter to the mayor! Remember to tell why it's a good idea for everyone.

Your Turn

Write a personal essay in one paragraph. Explain how you would solve or have solved a problem. It may be a problem in your school or community. Write as if you are speaking directly to your audience and grab their attention with a strong opening. Use the Writer's Checklist to check your writing.

Writer's Checklist

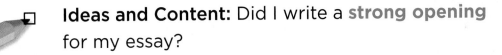

☐ **Ideas and Content:** Did I write a **strong opening** for my essay?

☑ **Organization:** Do the beginning sentences tell my problem and get the reader's attention?

☑ **Voice:** Did I address my audience directly?

☑ **Word Choice:** Did I use the right words to tell what happened?

☑ **Sentence Fluency:** Did I use different kinds of sentences for variety?

☑ **Conventions:** Did I use the correct forms of irregular verbs? Did I check my spelling?

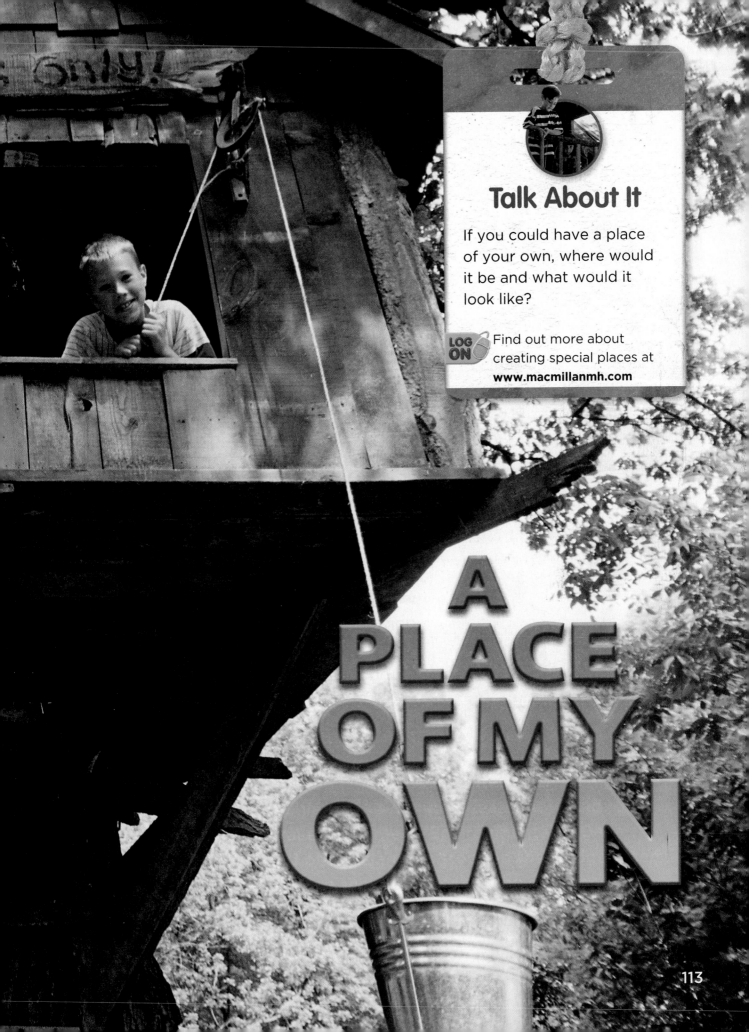

Talk About It

If you could have a place of your own, where would it be and what would it look like?

LOG ON Find out more about creating special places at **www.macmillanmh.com**

A PLACE OF MY OWN

Vocabulary

separate	exact
determination	ruined
storage	luckiest
crate	

Word Parts

Inflectional Endings

-*er* and -*est* show comparison. The ending -*er* means "more." The ending -*est* means "most."

luckiest = most lucky

Pond Street Clubhouse

by Sylvia Medrano

On Saturday I went to the lumberyard with Dad to order lumber for the new garage. I saw the wood and got an idea.

"Hey, Dad," I said. "Could we build a clubhouse?"

"Probably not," said Dad. "I'll be too busy with the garage."

"But Dad," I said, "you had a clubhouse when you were young."

Dad said, "I know, but first we have to build the garage."

I had to think of a way to get Dad to agree. "We can **separate** the clubhouse into two rooms," I said with **determination**. "One can be used as a **storage** room."

Dad thought about it for a moment. Then he said, "Let's wait to see if there is enough extra wood."

The garage supplies came the following weekend. There were huge piles of wood and a big box. It was a **crate** of nails and shingles for the roof. It looked like more than enough. When the truck left, Dad said, "Good news! We'll be able to build your clubhouse with the leftover wood when the garage is finished."

After a few weeks, it was time to start. A bunch of neighborhood kids came to help.

Dad let us measure the wood. Measuring has to be **exact** or else the pieces won't fit together. If Dad cut the wood too long or too short, our plans could be **ruined**. I knew we couldn't buy any extra wood.

When the clubhouse was finally finished, I was so thrilled. I made a sign and nailed it on the door. It said, "Pond Street Clubhouse—Welcome!" Now I have a great place to play. Am I the **luckiest** kid in town, or what?

Reread for **Comprehension**

Monitor Comprehension
Make and Confirm Predictions
You can monitor your comprehension of a story by making predictions about what characters might do or what events might take place. As you read on, check to see if your predictions were correct.

A Predictions Chart helps you monitor your understanding of what takes place in the story. Reread the story to make and confirm predictions.

What I Predict	What Happens

115

Comprehension

Genre

Realistic Fiction is an invented story that could have happened in real life.

Monitor Comprehension

Make and Confirm Predictions

As you read, use your Predictions Chart.

What I Predict	What Happens

Read to Find Out

Will the girl ever get her own room?

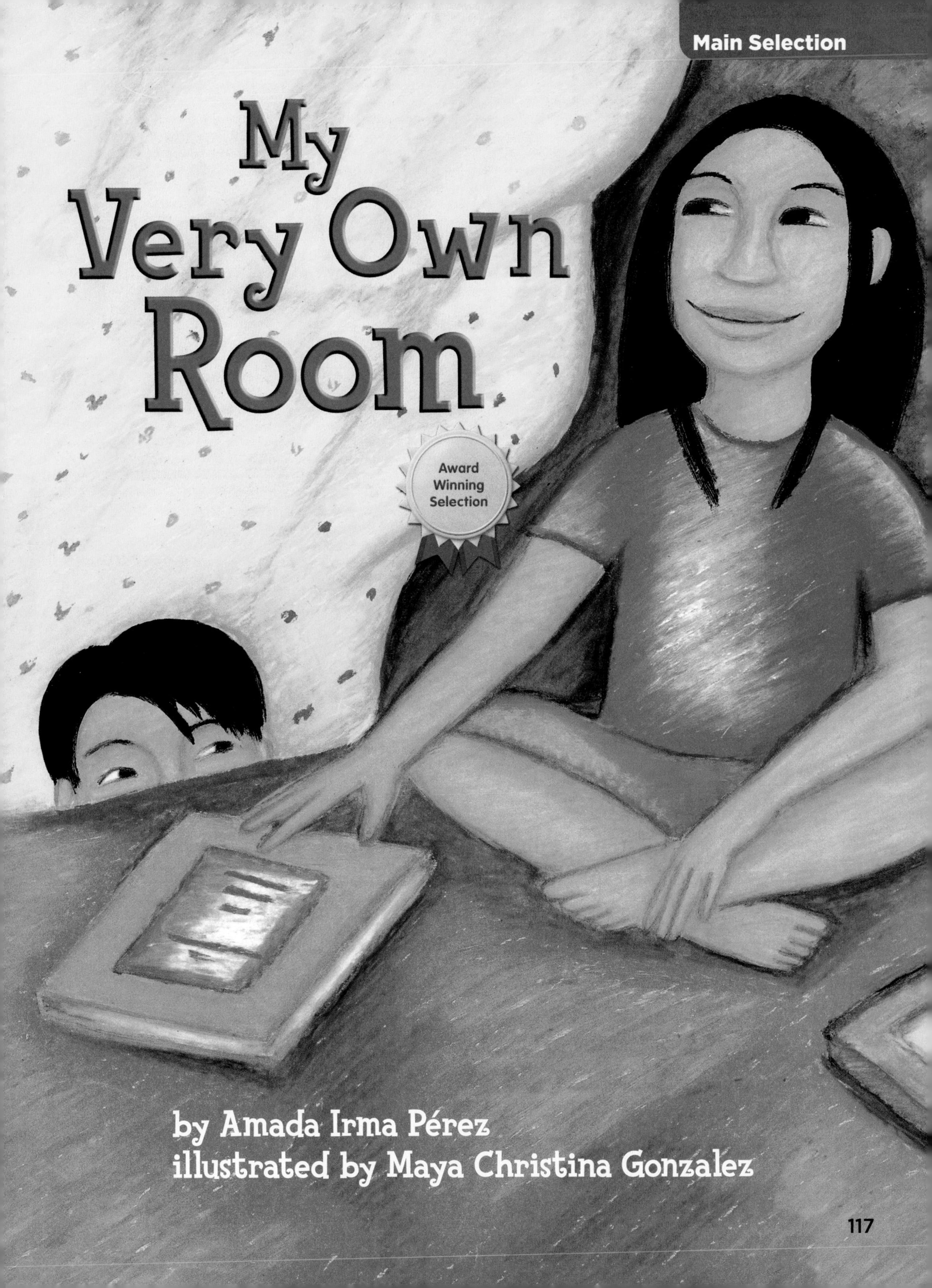

My Very Own Room

Award Winning Selection

by Amada Irma Pérez

illustrated by Maya Christina Gonzalez

I woke up one morning on a crowded bed in a crowded room. Víctor's elbow was jabbing me in the ribs. Mario had climbed out of his crib and crawled in with us. Now his leg lay across my face and I could hardly breathe. In the bed next to ours my three other brothers were sleeping.

I was getting too big for this. I was almost nine years old, and I was tired of sharing a room with my five little brothers. More than anything in the whole world I wanted a room of my own.

A little space was all I wanted, but there wasn't much of it. Our tiny house was shared by eight of us, and sometimes more when our friends and relatives came from Mexico and stayed with us until they found jobs and places to live.

Once a family with eight kids (mostly boys!) lived with us for two months. It was noisy and a lot of fun. There was always a long line to use the bathroom, but the toilet seat was always warm.

Sometimes very early in the morning while everyone was still sleeping, I would climb up the crooked ladder that leaned against the elm tree in our backyard. I would sit on a little board, pretending it was a bench, and just think. I could hear my father snoring. He worked all night at the factory and went to bed just before dawn.

I loved my brothers. It wasn't that I didn't want to be near them. I just needed a place of my own.

121

I tiptoed around our tiny, two bedroom house. I peeked behind the curtain my mother had made from flour sacks to **separate** our living room from the **storage** closet.

"Aha! This is it! This could be my room." I imagined it with my own bed, table, and lamp—a place where I could read the books I loved, write in my diary, and dream.

I sat down among the boxes. My mother must have heard me because she came in from the kitchen.

Make Predictions
What will the girl try to do with the storage closet?

"Mamá, it's perfect," I said, and I told her my idea.

"Ay, *mijita*, you do not understand. We are storing my sister's sewing machine and your uncle's garden tools. Someday they will need their things to make a better living in this new country. And there's the furniture and old clothes," she said. Slowly she shook her head.

After breakfast we started pushing the old furniture out to the back porch. Everyone helped. We were like a mighty team of powerful ants.

We carried furniture, tools, and machines. We dragged bulging bags of old clothes and toys. We pulled boxes of treasures and overflowing junk. Finally, everything was out except for a few cans of leftover paint from the one time we had painted the house.

126

Each can had just a tiny bit of paint inside. There was pink and blue and white, but not nearly enough of any one color to paint the room.

"I have an idea," I said to my brothers. "Let's mix them!" Héctor and Sergio helped me pour one can into another and we watched the colors swirl together. A new color began to appear, a little like purple and much stronger than pink. Magenta!

We painted and painted until we ran out of paint.

Mamá showed me how to measure my new magenta wall with a piece of bright yellow yarn left over from the last baby blanket she had crocheted. Tío Pancho was going back to Mexico and said I could have his bed, but we had to let him know if it would fit.

We cut off the piece of yarn that showed us just how big the bed could be. We all ran to Tío Pancho's waving the piece of yarn. We measured his bed. Perfect! That yellow piece of yarn was magical.

A little later Tío Pancho arrived with my new bed tied to the roof of his car. I ran out and hugged him. Papá helped him carry the bed in and carefully ease it into place.

My brothers jumped up and down and everybody clapped. Then Raúl moved an empty wooden **crate** over to my new bed and stood it on end to make a bedside table.

"All you need now is a little lamp," my mother said.

She brought out a shoe box stuffed with Blue Chip stamps she had been collecting for years. Mamá and Papá got them for free when they bought food or gas. They were like little prizes that could be used as money at special stores. But before we could spend them, we had to paste them into special stamp books.

We licked and licked and pasted and pasted. When we were done, Papá drove us to the stamp store.

Make Predictions
What will the girl do with the Blue Chip stamps?

131

An Encyclopedia Article

Reading an Encyclopedia Article

Encyclopedia articles are arranged alphabetically in each volume, or book.

page number   **guide word**   **caption**

503   Architecture

The Guggenheim Museum was designed by the architect Frank Lloyd Wright (1867-1959).

heading ➔ **Architecture**

Architecture is the art of designing buildings. An architect is a person who designs buildings and checks to make sure they are built correctly. Architects build many different kinds of buildings, including homes, schools, office buildings, skyscrapers, and monuments.

Early architecture

Architecture began when people built the first homes. The architecture of the ancient Egyptians included giant pyramids that were built for kings. Ancient Greeks were known for the beautiful stone columns of their early temples and monuments.

This article is from Volume A of an encyclopedia.

Later Years

Wright designed both the Guggenheim Museum in New York City and the Marin County Civic Center in California at the end of his career. He died in Arizona in 1959 before either of the buildings opened.

The ideas and work of Frank Lloyd Wright are **preserved**, or kept, by The Frank Lloyd Wright Foundation. The Foundation watches over his designs, drawings, writings, and his homes in Arizona and Wisconsin.

The Frank Lloyd Wright Foundation is located in Arizona.

Connect and Compare

1. Look at the encyclopedia article on Architecture on page 142. What do you think the numbers in parentheses mean? **Reading an Encyclopedia Article**

2. If you could travel back to the early 1900s to meet Frank Lloyd Wright, what questions would you ask him? **Apply**

3. Think about this article and *My Very Own Room*. Why might the narrator of the story enjoy learning about Frank Lloyd Wright? **Reading/Writing Across Texts**

Social Studies Activity

Find out more about a famous building such as the Eiffel Tower or the Sydney Opera House. Find out who the architect was and when the building was built.

Find out more about architecture at **www.macmillanmh.com**

Writer's Craft

Time-Order Words

Words such as *first*, *next*, *then*, and *last* tell the order in which things happen. Writers use these **time-order words** to show the sequence in which things should be done.

Write Directions

I used time-order words to show the sequence in which things should be done.

I completed my directions with the time-order word "last."

How to Make a Study Place

by Robert H.

Studying for a test is easier when you have a quiet place of your own. This is how to make one. First, find a chair that's comfortable and put it in a quiet corner that isn't too close to the TV, radio, or phone. Next, get a healthful snack so you'll think about studying, not dinner. Then, gather the materials you'll need. The last thing to do is to tell everyone in the house that you need peace and quiet.

144

Your Turn

Write a paragraph that explains how to do something. Choose something you know how to do well. Maybe you know how to ride a bike safely, make a sandwich, or give a party. Be sure to use time-order words such as *first*, *next*, *then*, and *last* to show the correct sequence of steps. Use the Writer's Checklist to check your writing.

Writer's Checklist

 Ideas and Content: Did I write about something I know?

 Organization: Did I write the steps in order?

 Voice: Does it sound like I know my topic well?

Word Choice: Did I use **time-order words** such as *first*, *next*, *then*, and *last*?

 Sentence Fluency: Does my writing sound good when it's read aloud?

 Conventions: Did I use contractions correctly? Did I check my spelling?

Test Strategy

Author and Me

The answer is not directly stated. Connect the clues to figure it out.

Susan B. Anthony:
A Pioneer for Women's Rights

by Maja James

SUSAN B. ANTHONY was born on February 15, 1820 to a Quaker family. Quakers believe that everyone should be treated fairly. In meetings, Quaker girls got up and spoke just as the boys did. Women could vote on church matters. Anthony's parents made sure that their daughters got a good education.

The freedoms Anthony had might not seem strange today. However, in the early 1800s, girls were not given an equal education and women could not own property.

In 1851 Anthony met Elizabeth Cady Stanton. They became close friends and leaders in the women's suffrage movement. The suffrage movement tried to get women the right to vote. They believed that "all men and women were created equal."

Susan B. Anthony

Go On ▶

Anthony and Stanton were a great team. Anthony was a good speaker, and she never gave up a fight. Stanton was a great thinker and writer, and she knew the law.

Anthony and Stanton wanted to change the United States Constitution to give women the right to vote.

Elizabeth Cady Stanton

In 1872 Anthony brought 15 women to vote in a national election. She was arrested. At her trial the courtroom was packed with reporters. The judge didn't let the jury decide Anthony's case. Instead, the judge said that Anthony did not have the right to vote. He charged her a $100 fine. She refused to pay.

Anthony continued to work for women's suffrage. She made many trips across the country and spoke about why women's rights were important. At home Anthony organized suffrage campaigns. Volunteers would sleep on every bed, sofa, and floor in her house.

During her life Anthony published several newspapers. She also wrote a book with Elizabeth Stanton and Matilda Gage about the suffrage movement.

Susan B. Anthony died in 1906. In 1920 the 19th Amendment was finally passed. It gave women the right to vote. This law is sometimes called the Susan B. Anthony Amendment.

Encyclopedia Article

Women's Suffrage Movement

The women's suffrage movement helped give women the right to vote. Although women now have the same voting rights as men, they did not get those rights until the early 1900s and they had to fight hard to get them. Men and women who supported the movement to give women the right to vote were called suffragists.

The movement begins. A changing society during the early 1800s and the fight for equality among all people led to the start of the women's suffrage movement. It was at this time that women started to get more education and to take part in politics. Women soon began to question why the law would not let them vote.

Go On ▶

Tip

Connect the clues or ideas from the passage to choose the best answer.

Directions: Answer the Questions.

1. **How do you know Susan B. Anthony's parents were important in forming her character?**

    A Her parents did not believe in educating girls.

    B She was only allowed to take an interest in her parents' causes.

    C She heard many speakers at her parents' house.

    D Her parents were Quakers who encouraged girls to speak out.

2. **What does the word *movement* mean in this selection?**

    A moving from place to place

    B a series of events

    C a sudden change

    D the actions of a group to gain a goal

3. **How is Susan B. Anthony described in history books?**

    A as an uneducated, but talented, speaker

    B as a famous criminal

    C as a leader in getting women the right to vote

    D as a woman who named an amendment after herself

4. **What information in the encyclopedia article is NOT included in Susan B. Anthony's biography?**

5. **Why was Susan B. Anthony's work important? Include examples from the selection in your answer.**

    ## Writing Prompt

    Write step-by-step directions to explain how to hold an election for class president.

Talk About It

How would you make money if you needed to buy something?

 Find out more about money at **www.macmillanmh.com**

MAKING MONEY

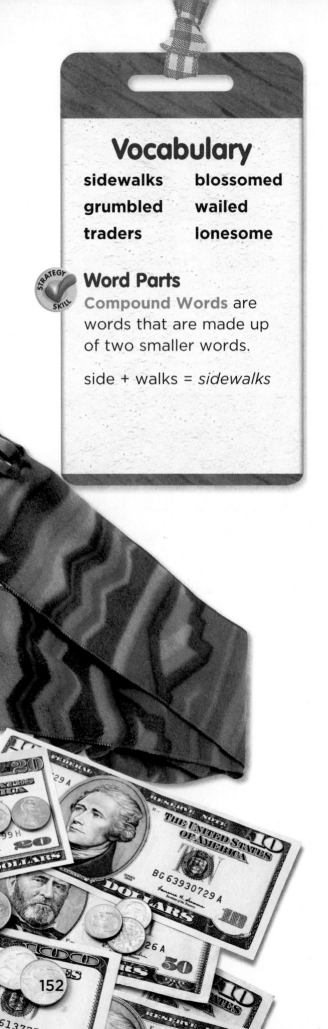

Vocabulary

sidewalks	blossomed
grumbled	wailed
traders	lonesome

STRATEGY SKILL

Word Parts

Compound Words are words that are made up of two smaller words.

side + walks = *sidewalks*

Let's Trade!

by Alex Ely

Elizabeth and Danny walked along newly paved **sidewalks** on a frosty winter morning. Elizabeth wore a hat and gloves but no scarf. Danny wore a hat and two scarves, but he didn't have any gloves. Both of them were freezing.

"I'm so cold," Elizabeth **grumbled** under her breath.

"Me too," Danny **wailed**.

Then Elizabeth had an idea! "What if I traded you one glove for one of your scarves?" Elizabeth said. "Then both of our necks would be warm, and we'd each have one warm hand. We could put the other hand in our pockets."

"Good idea!" said Danny.

After they shared the scarf and glove, they began to feel warmer.

A few minutes later Mrs. Baxter appeared. "Did I just see you barter?" she asked.

Elizabeth and Danny looked puzzled. "What's barter?" Elizabeth asked.

"Barter means trade," Mrs. Baxter explained. "You two traded a scarf and a glove so you could be warm. Did you know that **traders** bartered for thousands of years?"

"Really? How did it work?" Danny asked.

Mrs. Baxter said, "Well, traders who had too much of one thing, such as salt or cloth or pigs, would exchange them with other traders for other things that they needed. Trading grew and **blossomed**, but it had problems."

"Like what?" Elizabeth asked.

"Suppose you raised chickens. You could trade the chickens and eggs for what you needed. But if the chickens got away—"

"I wouldn't have anything to trade!"

"Exactly!" said Mrs. Baxter.

"And you'd be so **lonesome** without your poultry friends!" Danny said with a grin.

"Now you see why people began to use money to trade," Mrs. Baxter said.

"Is it true that silver and gold coins were used before paper money?" Danny asked.

"Yes, but they were too heavy to carry." Mrs. Baxter said. "People then began to write promises on paper instead of trading coins. That was how paper money got its start."

"Wow!" said Elizabeth, "but I guess people still trade sometimes, the way Danny and I did today!"

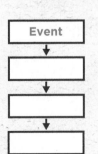

Reread for **Comprehension**

Summarize
Sequence

The sequence of events in a story is the order in which things take place. You can summarize the sequence of events in a story by paying close attention to when events happen.

A Sequence Chart helps you summarize story events in time order. Reread the story to find the order in which things happened.

Event
↓
↓
↓

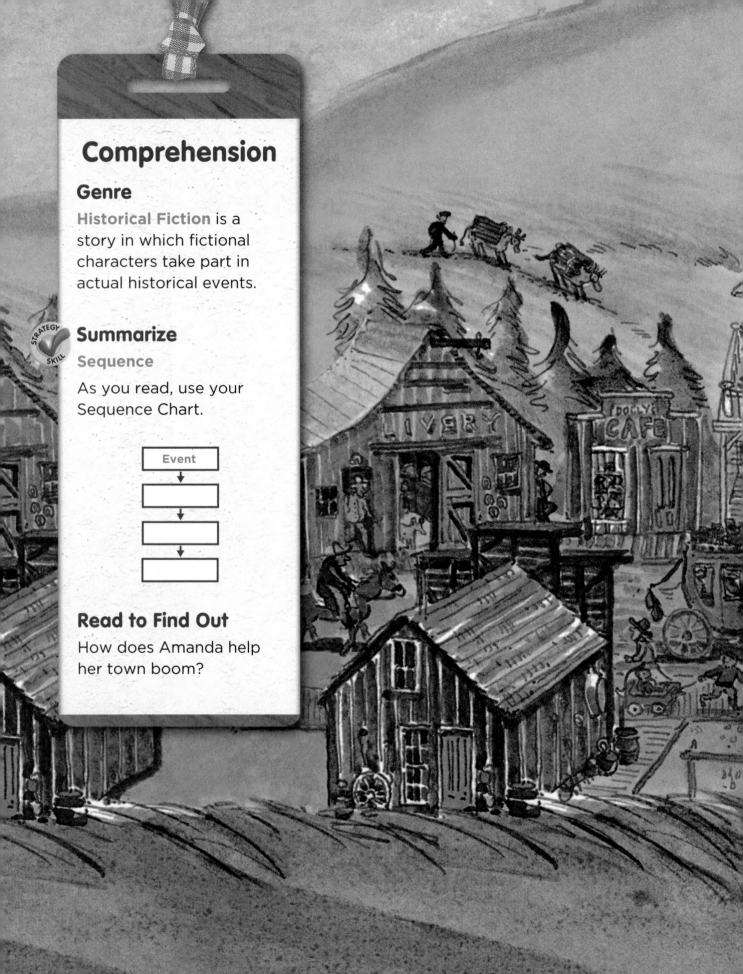

Comprehension

Genre

Historical Fiction is a story in which fictional characters take part in actual historical events.

Summarize

STRATEGY SKILL

Sequence

As you read, use your Sequence Chart.

Event
↓
↓
↓

Read to Find Out

How does Amanda help her town boom?

BOOM TOWN

by Sonia Levitin

illustrated by Cat Bowman Smith

Award Winning Author

It took us twenty-one days on the stagecoach to get
to California. When we got there, I thought we'd live with
Pa in the gold fields. A whole tent city was built up. But Ma
shook her head. "The gold fields are no place for children.
We'll get a cabin and live in town."

What town? A stage stop, a pump house, a few log cabins—
that was all. It was so wide and **lonesome** out west, even my
shadow ran off.

Ma found a cabin big enough for all of us: Baby Betsy, brothers Billy, Joe, Ted, and me—Amanda. Pa came in from the gold fields every Saturday night, singing:

"So I got me a mule
And some mining tools,
A shovel and a pick and a pan;

But I work all day
Without no pay.
I guess I'm a foolish man."

First Ma made him take a bath in a tin tub set out under the stars. Then Pa sang songs and told stories he'd heard from the miners—stories about men finding big nuggets and striking it rich. But poor Pa, he had no luck at all. Still, every Monday morning he'd leave for the gold fields full of hope.

Days were long and lonely. The hills spread out as far as forever. Nights, me and Ma and my brothers and Baby Betsy would sit out and wait for a shooting star to sail across the sky. Once in a while a crow flew by. That's all the excitement there was.

My brothers worked up some furrows. They planted corn and potatoes and beans. Then they ran around climbing trees, skinning their knees. But after all the water was fetched and the wash was done, after the soap was made and the fire laid, after the beds were fixed and the floor was swept clean, I'd sit outside our cabin door with Baby Betsy, so bored I thought I'd die. Also, I hankered for some pie. I loved to bake pie.

I asked Ma and she said, "Pie would be good, but we have no pie pans and no real oven, just the wood stove. How would you bake a pie?"

I poked around in a big box of stuff and found an old iron skillet. I decided to make a pie crust and pick gooseberries to fill it.

Gooseberries grew on the bushes near town. I picked a big pailful and went back home. I made a crust with flour, butter, a little water, and a pinch of salt, and then I rolled it out.

Ma came in and said, "Looks good, Amanda. I knew you could make it. But tell me, how will you bake it?"

I showed Ma the skillet. She shook her head. "I don't think it will work, but you can try."

"It will work," I said.

Sequence

What steps does Amanda take to start baking her pie?

Brothers Billy and Joe and Ted stood there laughing. When the wood turned to coals, I pushed my pie inside the old stove. After a while I smelled a bad burning. I pulled out my pie, hard as a rock. Billy, Joe, and Ted whooped and slapped their sides. They snatched up my pie and tossed it high into the air. They ran outside and Billy whacked it hard with a stick. Pie pieces flew all over the place, and my brothers bent over, laughing.

I was so mad I went right back in to make another, and I swore none of them would get a bite. I rolled out my crust and filled it with berries, shoved the pie into the oven, and soon took it out.

I set the pie down to cool. I went off to do some mending. Next thing I knew, Baby Betsy, just learning to walk, sat there with pie goo all over her face. Too soft, the filling ran down on Betsy, and she **wailed** like a coyote in the night.

It took one more try, but I got it right. That night we ate my gooseberry pie, and it was delicious.

When Pa came home from the gold fields on Saturday night, there was a pie for him, too. "Amanda, you are the queen of the kitchen!" Pa scooped me up and whirled me around. I was proud.

The next week I made an extra pie for Pa to take with him to the gold fields.

Saturday night when he came home singing, coins jangled in his pocket.

We all ran out to ask, "Did you strike gold, Pa?"

"No," he said. "I sold Amanda's pie. The miners loved it. They paid me twenty-five cents a slice!"

After that, Pa took pies to the gold fields every week. And every week he came home with coins in his pockets. Some miners walked right to our door looking for pie. They told Ma, "You should open a bakery."

Ma said, "It's my girl Amanda who is the baker. If she wants to make pies, that's fine. But I have no time."

Ma had a new baby on the way. It was up to me. I figured I could sell pies to the miners and fill up our money jar.

But I needed help. I rounded up my brothers and told them, "If you want to eat pie, you've got to work."

They **grumbled** and groaned, but they knew I meant it. So Billy built me a shelf, Joe made a sign, AMANDA'S FINE PIES, and Ted helped pick berries and sour apples.

I needed more pans and another bucket. One day Peddler Pete came by, and with the money I'd made I bought them.

"You're a right smart little girl," said the peddler, "being in business like this."

I thought fast and told him, "Anybody can make money out here. Folks need things all the time, and there're no stores around. If you were to settle and start one, I'll bet you'd get rich."

Peddler Pete scratched his beard. "Not a bad idea," he said. "My feet are sore from roaming. I could use this cart and build my way up to having a store."

So pretty soon we had us a real store called PEDDLER PETE'S TRADING POST. Trappers and **traders** and travelers appeared. After shopping at Pete's, they were good and hungry.

They came to our cabin, looking for pie. Some liked it here so well they decided to stay. Soon we had a cooper, a tanner, a miller, a blacksmith. A town was starting to grow.

A prospector came in on the stage from St. Joe, his clothes covered with dirt. He looked around at the folks eating pie, and he asked, "Is there someone here who does washing?"

I stepped right up and I told him, "What we need is a laundry. Why don't you stay and start one? Why, the miners are sending their shirts clear to China. You'll make more money doing laundry than looking for gold."

The man thought a while, then said with a smile, "You're right, little lady. It's a dandy idea. I'll send for my wife to help."

Soon shirts and sheets fluttered on the line as people brought their washing in. A tailor came to make and mend clothes. A cobbler crafted shoes and boots. We heard the *tap tap* of his hammer and smelled the sweet leather. A barber moved in with shaving mugs, and an apothecary with herbs and healing drugs. So the town grew up all around us.

My pie business **blossomed**. Sometimes the line snaked clear around the house. Baby Betsy entertained the people while they waited. Billy added another shelf. Joe and Ted made a bench. We all picked berries and apples. Even Ma came to help. We had to get a bigger jar for all the money coming in.

One day our old friend Cowboy Charlie rode by. Like everyone else, he stopped for some pie. "I'd like to rest a spell," he said. "Where can I leave my horse for the night?"

"There's no livery stable," I said. "But why don't you start one? You'd rent out horses, and wagons too. That would be the perfect business for you."

"You're just full of great ideas, little lady," Cowboy Charlie said. He twirled his lariat. "I'd like to settle down. I'll stay here and do just that."

Soon a trail was worn right to Charlie's stable door. All day we heard the snorting of horses. Now Charlie needed hay. Farmers brought wagons and sacks full of feed. With all those people riding in, someone decided to build a hotel and a cafe. The town grew fast all around us.

The owner of the cafe bought pies from me, five or six at a time. I taught Billy how to roll the crust. Joe got wood for the stove. Ted washed the fruit, and Baby Betsy tried to stir in the sugar.

The money jar in our kitchen looked ready to bust. Where could we safely keep all that cash? Lucky us, one day Mr. Hooper, the banker, appeared.

"I'm building a bank," Mr. Hooper said to me. "This is getting to be a boom town."

"We'll use your bank," I told Mr. Hooper, "but the roads are so poor. In winter there's mud, and in summer there's dust. We need some **sidewalks** and better streets."

"You're a smart little lady," said Mr. Hooper, tipping his hat. "I'll see what I can do about that."

Before we knew it, the bank was built and wooden sidewalks were laid. One street was called Bank Street; the other was Main. Soon every lane and landmark had a name. Pa and my brothers built on a big room for our bakery.

Men sent for their families. New houses appeared everywhere. Babies and children filled up the town. We needed a school, and a good schoolmarm.

We knew Miss Camilla from our stagecoach days. She was living up the coast a ways. Cowboy Charlie rode off to fetch her, and she was glad to come.

Miss Camilla, the teacher, had married a preacher, and he came too. We all got together to build a church and a school. Bells rang out every day of the week. Now this was a real boom town!

One day Pa said to me, "Amanda, I'm through panning for gold. Will you let me be in business with you?"

"Sure!" I said, happily. "I'd love to work with you, Pa, and I'd also like to go to school."

Sequence
What sequence of events takes place to create this boom town?

So Pa turned to baking, and we all worked together. Pa sang while he rolled out the dough:

"Amanda found a skillet
And berries to fill it,
Made pies without a pan;

Our pies are the best
In all the West.
I guess I'm a lucky man."

Now Pa is with us every day. There's excitement and bustle all around. Our house sits in the middle of a boom town!

174

And to think it all started with me, Amanda, baking pies!

BANK ON SONIA AND CAT

AUTHOR
Sonia Levitin wrote this story after reading about a woman who made more than $10,000 by baking pies in a skillet during the California Gold Rush. Sonia loves research, so it is not surprising that she found such an interesting fact. History is just one of the things that Sonia likes to write about. She also writes mysteries, adventures, and funny stories.

ILLUSTRATOR
Cat Bowman Smith started out drawing magazine pictures. Her illustrations became very popular. Soon she was illustrating books. Today she has illustrated more than 40 of them.

 Find out more about Sonia Levitin and Cat Bowman Smith at **www.macmillanmh.com**

Other books by Sonia Levitin: *Nine for California* and *Taking Charge*

Author's Purpose
Did Sonia Levitin write to inform or entertain readers? What clues help you figure out her purpose?

Comprehension Check

 STRATEGY SKILL

Summarize

Use your Sequence Chart to help you summarize *Boom Town.* Retell the story's events in the order in which they happen.

Event
↓
↓
↓

Think and Compare

 STRATEGY SKILL

1. Tell about two things that happened after Amanda's pie business **blossomed**. Use story details in your answer. **Summarize: Sequence**

2. Reread pages 162-163 of *Boom Town.* From those two pages, what conclusions can you draw about the kind of person Amanda is? Use story details to support your answer. **Analyze**

3. If you start your own business, what information from the story could help you to be successful? Explain. **Apply**

4. Based on this story, do you think new businesses are important to the growth of a town or a city? Use examples from the story. Explain. **Evaluate**

5. Read "Let's Trade" on pages 152-153. Compare how the characters in "Let's Trade!" and *Boom Town* got the things that they needed. **Reading/Writing Across Texts**

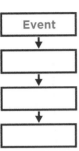

Social Studies

Genre

Nonfiction Articles give information about real people, places, or things.

Text Feature

Calendars show the months, weeks, and days of the year.

SKILL

Content Vocabulary

business

services

batches

demand

How to Earn Money!

by R. J. Harkin

Would you like to do something new and exciting? Would you like to be looked up to and respected by kids and adults alike? Would you like to earn money in your free time? If you answered "Yes!" to any of these questions, then starting your own **business** might be right for you!

You Can Do It!

"My own business?" you might ask. "But I'm only a third-grader!" No problem! Even third-graders have plenty of talent and **services** to offer.

Do you enjoy cooking or baking? Then you may consider whipping up and selling a few **batches** of your fabulous blueberry muffins. Do you like arts and crafts? If so, why not make and sell artwork or jewelry? Do animals like you? Many busy families need responsible people to walk their dogs and feed their cats. The possibilities are endless! So, wash a car, plant a garden, or a lawn. If people want and need your special talents, you'll soon be in business!

Starting a Dog-Washing Business

 Using a Calendar

Before starting a business, you need to make a plan. A calendar can help you organize and keep track of what you need to do.

1. Find out if there is a **demand** for your business.

2. Advertise your business.

May

Sunday	Monday	Tuesday	Wednesday	Thursday	Friday	Saturday
				1 — Talk to neighbors.	2	3 →
4	5 — Make flyers.	6	7	8 →	9	10
11	12 — Put up flyers.	13	14	15	16	17 →
18	19	20	21	22	23	24 — Buy dog shampoo.
25	26	27 — Collect tubs and towels.	28	29	30 →	(31) Wash Dogs!

3. Gather materials and supplies.

4. Open your business.

Connect and Compare

1. Look at the calendar on page 180. How many days are scheduled for advertising? **Using a Calendar**

2. Suppose you live in a neighborhood where most people work all day. They aren't home to cook, work in the yard, or spend time with their pets. What businesses might there be a demand for? **Apply**

3. What advice do you think Amanda could give kids who may want to start a business today? **Reading/Writing Across Texts**

Social Studies Activity

Research a business that interests you. Create a calendar that shows your preparations for opening that business.

 Find out more about businesses at **www.macmillanmh.com**

Writer's Craft

Multiple Paragraphs

When writing **multiple paragraphs**, make sure the paragraphs go in a logical order. Each paragraph should begin with a topic sentence that states the main idea. The other sentences give supporting details.

The first topic sentence contrasts, and the second compares.

The details of each paragraph support the main idea of each topic sentence.

How Much Alike Are We?

by Sarah A.

Amanda and I are different because she lived a long time ago and I live in modern times. Amanda and her family traveled on a wagon. We have a minivan. She wears dresses. I wear jeans.

Amanda and I are also the same. We are girls who like to bake. Plus, Amanda started a pie business, and I walk dogs for the neighbors.

Amanda and I are probably more alike than we are different. We are both active people interested in many different things.

Your Turn

Write three paragraphs to compare and contrast life now with life when your parents were young. Use a Venn diagram to sort things that are alike and different. In one paragraph, compare things that are alike. In another paragraph, contrast differences. Sum up in a third paragraph. Use the Writer's Checklist to check your writing.

Writer's Checklist

 Ideas and Content: Is it clear from my writing how the people are alike and different?

 Organization: Do my **multiple paragraphs** go in a logical order? Does each paragraph start with a topic sentence?

 Voice: Does my writing sound like me?

 Word Choice: Did I use comparison words such as *same* and *different*?

 Sentence Fluency: Are my sentences too long?

 Conventions: Did I use pronouns correctly? Did I check my spelling?

An Armenian family with a cow

Helping People Help Themselves

by Zoe Tomasi

In the 1930s, Dan West was farming in Spain. It was wartime, and people were starving. As he handed out cups of milk to children, an idea hit him. "These children don't need a cup. They need a cow." This was the start of Heifer International.

Send Some Cows

Do you think a nice **gift** is a bike or CD? Heifer International gives different kinds of presents. Its presents might say "quack" or "moo." Dan West asked friends in the United States to give gifts of heifers, or young cows. Since then, Heifer International has given animals to four million families. It gives people the chance to feed themselves.

Pass on the Gift

Heifer International wants the people they help to help others. For one project, the group sent chickens to some children in Asia. The children **yearned** for the day when they could help others.

Nine-year-old Julie said, "I want other girls like me to take care of chickens and their families. I want to share and give many away."

Julie knew she had to **tend** to her chickens well so they would **produce** new eggs and healthy chicks. She took good care of them, and they gave birth to strong, **sturdy** chicks. Julie then passed on the gift of chicks to other families.

Letting Children Learn

Because of Heifer International, children can spend their days in a **schoolhouse** instead of working in the fields. They can use the money they earn from their animals to pay for school.

Heifer International has made a huge difference in people's lives for many years, thanks to a **kindhearted** farmer named Dan West.

This girl will care for her chicks so they grow up to be healthy.

Reread for **Comprehension**

Make Inferences and Analyze
Cause and Effect

Why something happens is the cause. What happens is the effect. Recognizing these two things can help you make inferences about what you are reading.

A Cause and Effect Chart helps you analyze what happened in a story and make inferences about why it happened. Reread the selection to find several effects and their causes.

Cause	→	Effect
	→	
	→	
	→	

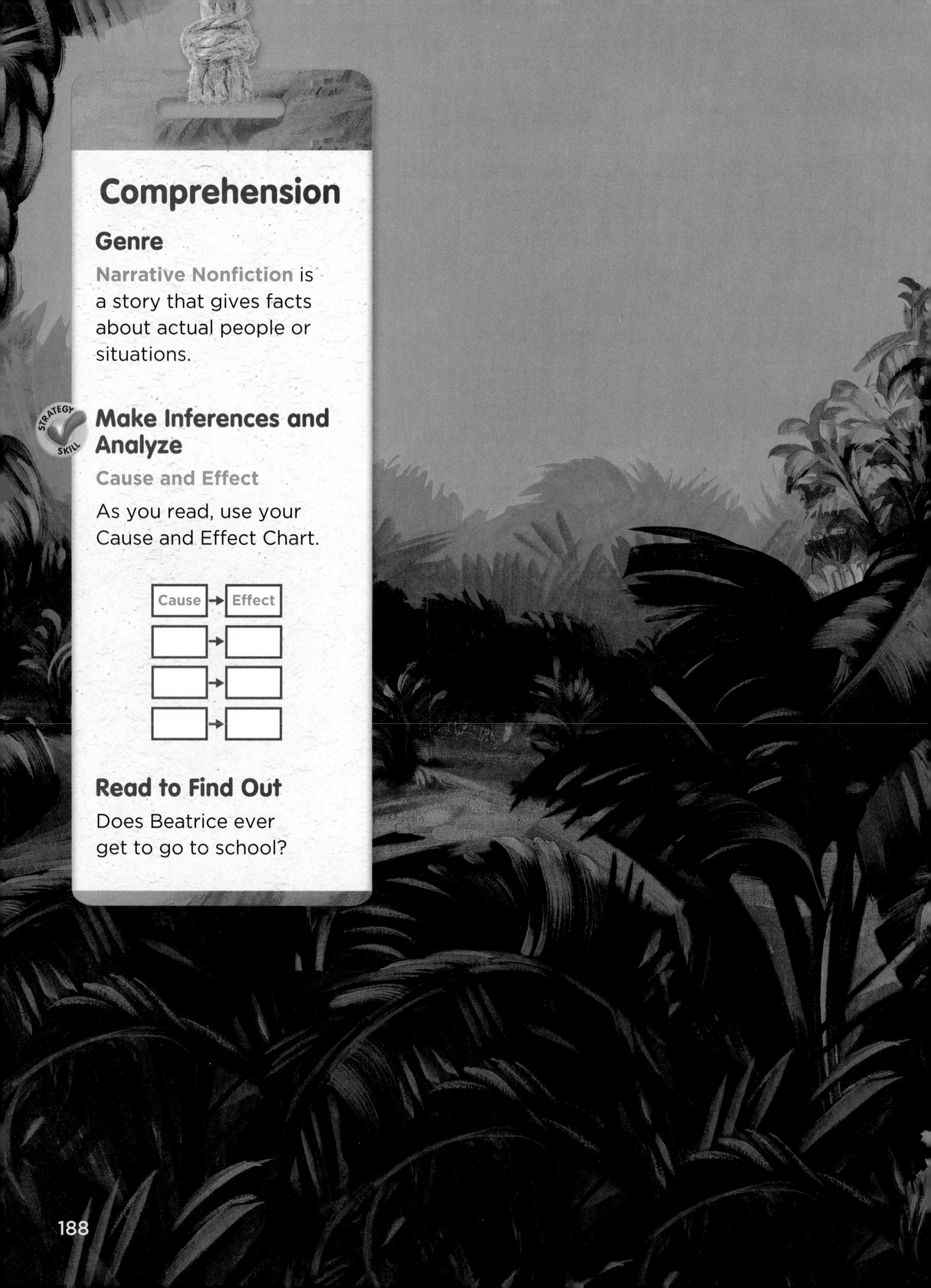

Comprehension

Genre

Narrative Nonfiction is a story that gives facts about actual people or situations.

Make Inferences and Analyze

Cause and Effect

As you read, use your Cause and Effect Chart.

Cause	→	Effect
	→	
	→	
	→	

Read to Find Out

Does Beatrice ever get to go to school?

188

Beatrice's Goat

by Page McBrier
illustrated by Lori Lohstoeter

Award Winning Author

If you were to visit the small African village of Kisinga in the rolling hills of western Uganda, and if you were to take a left at the crossroads and follow a narrow dirt path between two tall banana groves, you would come to the home of a girl named Beatrice.

Beatrice lives here with her mother and five younger brothers and sisters in a **sturdy** mud house with a fine steel roof. The house is new. So is the shiny blue wooden furniture inside. In fact, many things are new to Beatrice and her family lately.

And it's all because of a goat named Mugisa.

Beatrice loves everything about Mugisa . . . the feel of her coarse brown-and-white coat, the way her chin hairs curl just so, and how Mugisa gently teases her by butting her knobby horns against Beatrice's hand—*tup, tup*—like a drumbeat waiting for a song.

But there is one reason why Beatrice loves Mugisa most of all.

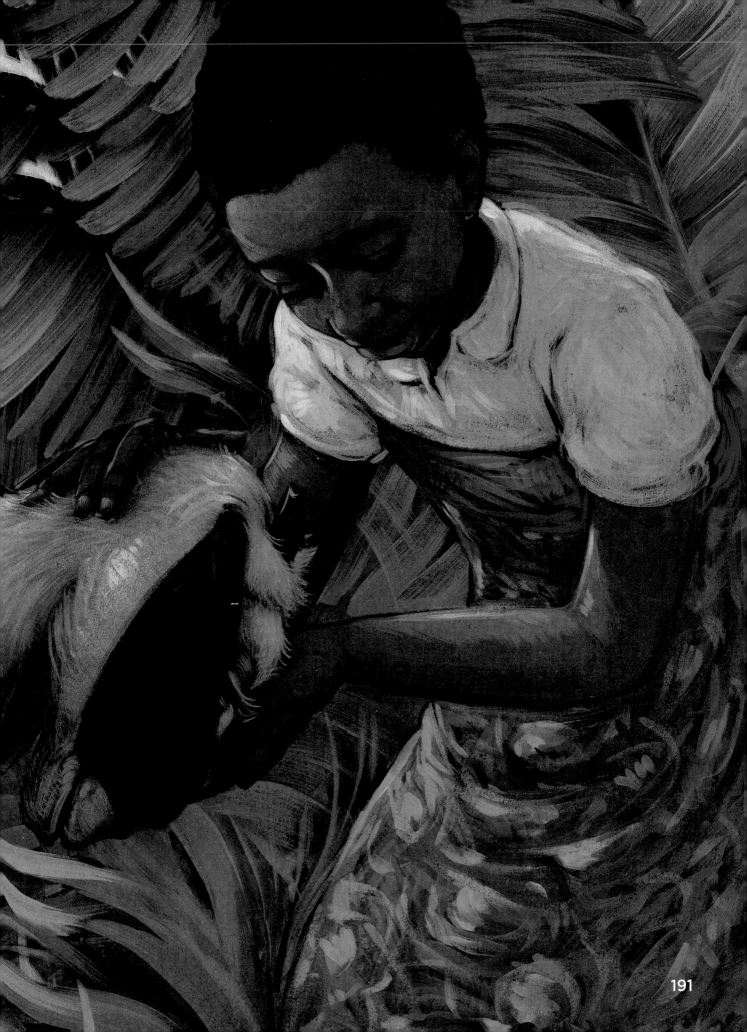

In the time before Mugisa, Beatrice spent her days helping her mama hoe and plant in the fields, **tend** the chickens, watch the younger children, and grind the cassava flour that they would take to market to sell.

Once in a while, when she was tending baby Paskavia, Beatrice would stop by the **schoolhouse**. Often, the students had carried their long wooden benches outside to work under the cool shade of the jackfruit trees. Then Beatrice would stand quietly off to one side, pretending she was a student, too.

Oh, how she longed to be a schoolgirl! How she **yearned** to sit on one of the benches and figure sums on a small slate chalkboard. How she wished to turn the pages of a worn copybook and study each word over and over until it stuck in her mind like a burr.

"I'll never be able to go to school," she would sigh. "How could I ever save enough money to pay for books or a uniform?"

One day while Beatrice was busy pulling weeds, Mama came to her with dancing eyes. "Beatrice, some **kindhearted** people from far away have given us a lucky **gift**. We are one of twelve village families to receive a goat."

Beatrice was puzzled. A goat? What kind of gift was a goat? It couldn't get up each morning and start their charcoal fire for cooking. It couldn't hike down to the stream each week and scrub their dirty clothes clean. It couldn't keep an eye on Grace, Moses, Harriet, Joash, and Paskavia.

Her long fingers tugged patiently at the weeds. "That's very nice, Mama," she said politely.

Then Mama added, "It will be your job to take care of our goat. If you do, it can bring wonderful things."

Beatrice looked up at her mother. "Will this goat come soon?" she asked. "Because I would like to meet such a goat."

Mama laughed. "Good things take time. First I must plant pastures and build our goat a shed."

Beatrice nodded slowly. Surely Mama knew what she was doing. "I will help you," she declared.

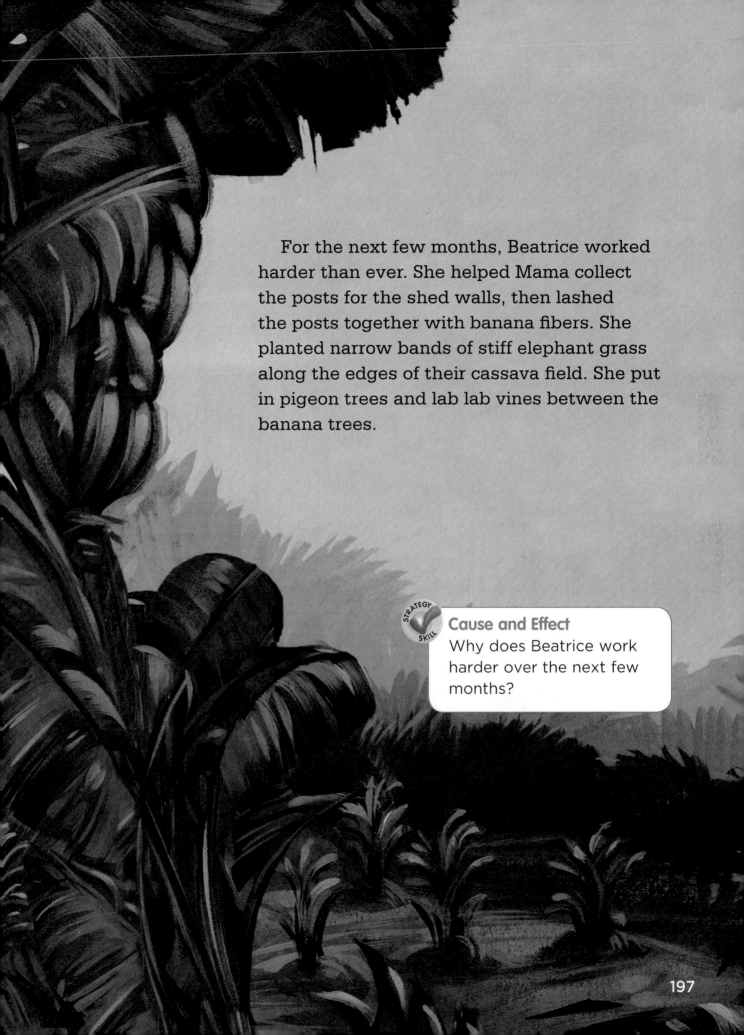

For the next few months, Beatrice worked harder than ever. She helped Mama collect the posts for the shed walls, then lashed the posts together with banana fibers. She planted narrow bands of stiff elephant grass along the edges of their cassava field. She put in pigeon trees and lab lab vines between the banana trees.

STRATEGY SKILL

Cause and Effect
Why does Beatrice work harder over the next few months?

Finally, one day Beatrice's goat arrived, fat and sleek as a ripe mango. Beatrice stood shyly with her brothers and sisters, then stepped forward and circled the goat once. She knelt close, inspecting its round belly, and ran her hand along its smooth back. "Mama says you are our lucky gift," she whispered. "So that is what I will name you. *Mugisa* ... luck."

Two weeks later, Mugisa gave birth. It was Beatrice who discovered first one kid and then, to her surprise, another. "Twins!" she exclaimed, stooping down to examine them. "See that, my Mugisa? You have already brought us *two* wonderful things." Beatrice named the first kid *Mulindwa*, which means expected, and the second *Kihembo*, or surprise.

Each day Beatrice made sure Mugisa got extra elephant grass and water to help her **produce** lots of milk, even though it meant another long trip down to the stream and back.

When the kids no longer needed it, Beatrice took her own first taste of Mugisa's milk. "Mmm. Sweet," she said, mixing the rest into her cup of breakfast porridge. Beatrice knew Mugisa's milk would keep them all much healthier.

One day, Beatrice returned from collecting water and noticed Mama frowning and counting the money in her woven purse. Beatrice put down the water can and rushed to her mother's side. "Mama! What is it?" she asked. "What's wrong?"

As she looked up, Mama's frown turned to a small smile. "I think," she said, "you may just have saved enough to pay for school."

"School?" Beatrice gasped in disbelief. "But what about all the other things we need?"

"First things first," Mama said.

Beatrice threw her arms around her mother's neck. "Oh, Mama, thank you." Then she ran to where her goat stood chewing her cud and hugged her tight. "Oh, Mugisa!" she whispered. "Today *I* am the lucky one. You have given me the gift I wanted most."

The very next week Beatrice started school. On the first morning that she was to attend, she sat proudly waiting for milk customers in her new yellow blouse and blue jumper, Mugisa by her side.

Beatrice felt nervous and excited at the same time. Mugisa pressed close, letting her coarse coat brush softly against Beatrice's cheek. "Oh, Mugisa," Beatrice cried. "I'll miss you today!"

Then she thought again about all the good things Mugisa was bringing. Mama said that soon Surprise would be sold for a lot of money. "It will be enough to tear down this old house," she had explained. "We will be able to put up a new one with a steel roof that won't leak during the rains."

Beatrice heard a rustle and noticed Bunane heading toward her with his empty milk pail. He eyed her new uniform and sighed. "You're so lucky. I wish *I* could go to school."

Beatrice reached out and touched Bunane's arm. "I've heard that your family is next in line to receive a goat."

A smile crossed Bunane's face. "Really?"

"Really."

Then Beatrice kissed Mugisa on the soft part of her nose, close to where her chin hairs curled just so, and started off to school.

Page and Lori's Story

AUTHOR

PAGE McBRIER was lucky enough to go to Uganda to meet Beatrice. She and Lori Lohstoeter had a six-hour drive to reach Beatrice's little village. After Page finished this story, she visited Beatrice again. By then, Beatrice had finished high school and was getting ready for college.

Other books by Page McBrier:
Oliver and the Lucky Duck and
The Treehouse Times

ILLUSTRATOR

LORI LOHSTOETER learned about Beatrice when she met someone from a special group that helps families. Lori wanted to draw the pictures for a book about Beatrice, but she needed to find someone to write the story. Lori asked Page, and they went to Africa to meet Beatrice and tell her story.

LOG ON Find out more about Page McBrier and Lori Lohstoeter at **www.macmillanmh.com**

Author's Purpose

Did Page McBrier want to entertain or persuade readers, or both? Identify the author's purpose (or purposes) and point to examples in the selection.

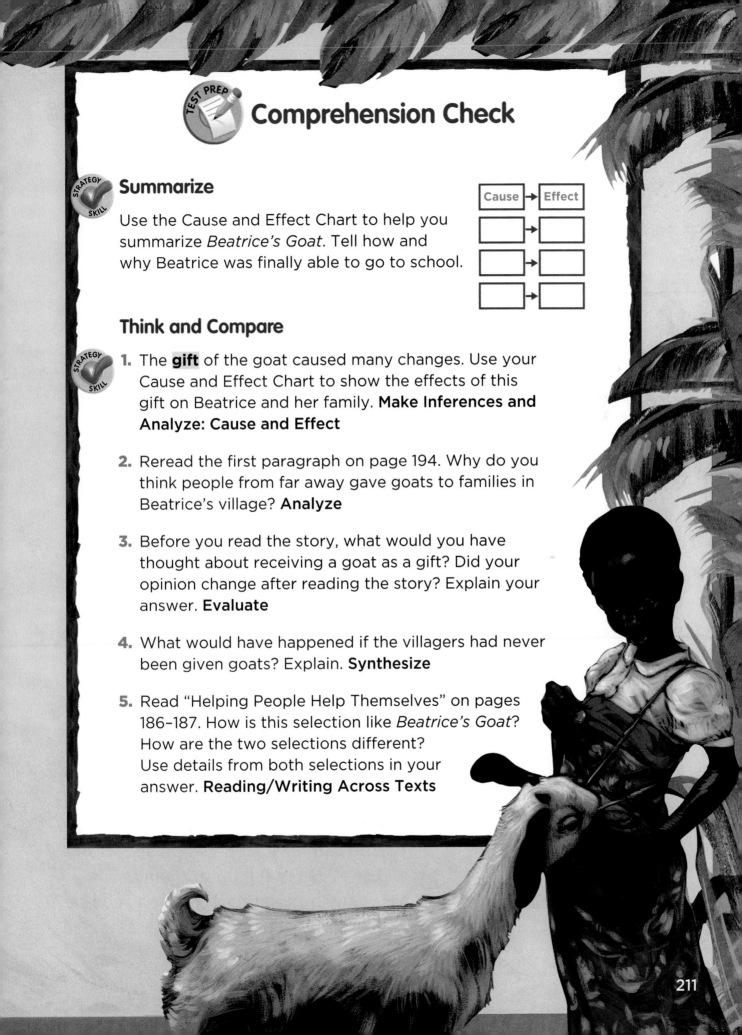

Comprehension Check

TEST PREP

Summarize

STRATEGY SKILL

Use the Cause and Effect Chart to help you summarize *Beatrice's Goat*. Tell how and why Beatrice was finally able to go to school.

Cause	→	Effect
	→	
	→	
	→	

Think and Compare

STRATEGY SKILL

1. The **gift** of the goat caused many changes. Use your Cause and Effect Chart to show the effects of this gift on Beatrice and her family. **Make Inferences and Analyze: Cause and Effect**

2. Reread the first paragraph on page 194. Why do you think people from far away gave goats to families in Beatrice's village? **Analyze**

3. Before you read the story, what would you have thought about receiving a goat as a gift? Did your opinion change after reading the story? Explain your answer. **Evaluate**

4. What would have happened if the villagers had never been given goats? Explain. **Synthesize**

5. Read "Helping People Help Themselves" on pages 186–187. How is this selection like *Beatrice's Goat*? How are the two selections different? Use details from both selections in your answer. **Reading/Writing Across Texts**

Social Studies

Genre

Newspaper Articles tell about important people and events and are part of daily or weekly newspapers.

Text Feature

Editorials are newspaper articles that present the opinions of the publisher or editors. They try to persuade the reader to do or believe something.

Content Vocabulary

achieve

determined

encourages

Ugandan Girl Reaches Goal

by Ann Frost

To Beatrice Biira, getting an education is the most important goal a person can have. Even when she was a little girl growing up in Uganda, she saw how important it is to get a good education. A goat named Mugisa helped her **achieve**, or reach, that goal.

After receiving Mugisa from the charity group Heifer International, Beatrice's family took care of the goat and the goat's young, which are called kids. With the money they made from selling milk and one of the kids, the Biiras were able to buy things they needed. Many people would have been satisfied with that, but Beatrice wanted more. She wanted to go to school.

Ten-year-old Beatrice had to start first grade with much younger students. This just made her more **determined** to work harder. Soon she caught up with her friends. Beatrice's good grades made it possible for her to go to school in the United States.

Even though it was hard for Beatrice to live so far away from her family, it has been worth it to her to get a good education.

Beatrice feeds Mugisa.

213

About Beatrice

SKILL Reading an Editorial

Editorials contain facts, as well as the opinions of the publisher or editor.

The News

| Vol. 3 | LATE CITY EDITION | April 17, 2007 |

The title of a newspaper article or editorial is called the headline.

How Important Is Education? Ask Beatrice!

by Earl Clements, Jr.

This expresses an opinion.

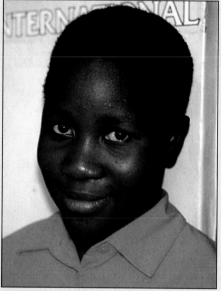

Getting an education should be one of the most important goals a person has. Beatrice Biira knew this when she was a little girl growing up in Uganda. Beatrice's family could not afford to buy the uniform and books she needed for school. When Heifer International gave her family a goat, Beatrice worked hard to take care of it and sell its milk. She earned enough money to buy books and a uniform. She worked hard at school and eventually went to college in the United States. Beatrice plans to help others reach their goals of getting an education and a better life.

Education has changed Beatrice Biira's life. She has appeared on television to tell her story and has visited schools to talk about how Mugisa the goat changed her life.

Beatrice worked hard. She didn't give up. Today, she **encourages**, or urges, students to read and help make the world a better place.

Beatrice visits classrooms to talk about her experiences.

Connect and Compare

1. Which sentences in the editorial express opinions? **Reading an Editorial**

2. Do you agree with the opinion in the editorial about the importance of education? Explain. **Evaluate**

3. Think about *Beatrice's Goat* and this article. Which parts let you know how Beatrice feels about getting an education? **Reading/Writing Across Texts**

Social Studies Activity

Find out about an organization, like Heifer International, that helps people. Write an editorial that tries to convince people to donate money or time to that organization.

Find out more about charitable organizations at **www.macmillanmh.com**

215

Writer's Craft

Transition Words

Good writers use **transition words** to connect ideas. Words such as *because* and *as a result* help show cause and effect.

The words "as a result" explain what happened when Bert started to crawl.

I used the word "because" to explain why I understand Bert.

How Bert Changed My Life

by Danielle L.

Bert, my new baby brother, changed my life. I used to have my own room. Now Bert sleeps in my room in his crib. He likes to throw his stuffed animals on the floor. If I don't give them back to him, he cries. Now Bert can crawl. As a result, he knocks down my block castles and chews on my books! Because I know he is just a baby, I put my books on shelves and build new castles. Things change when you are a big sister!

Your Turn

Write a paragraph about someone or something that has changed your life. You can write about something you did. You can also tell about a person you know or have read about. Be sure to include transition words such as *because*. Use the Writer's Checklist to check your writing.

Writer's Checklist

 Ideas and Content: Did I include vivid details that tell about the topic?

 Organization: Did I write a good topic sentence?

 Voice: Did I show how I feel about the topic?

 Word Choice: Did I use **transition words** that help the reader connect my ideas?

 Sentence Fluency: Did I vary the kinds of sentences I used?

 Conventions: Did I use subject and object pronouns correctly? Did I check my spelling?

Talk About It

How many different ways can you think of that people get from one place to another?

 Find out more about movement and transportation at **www.macmillanmh.com**

IN MOTION

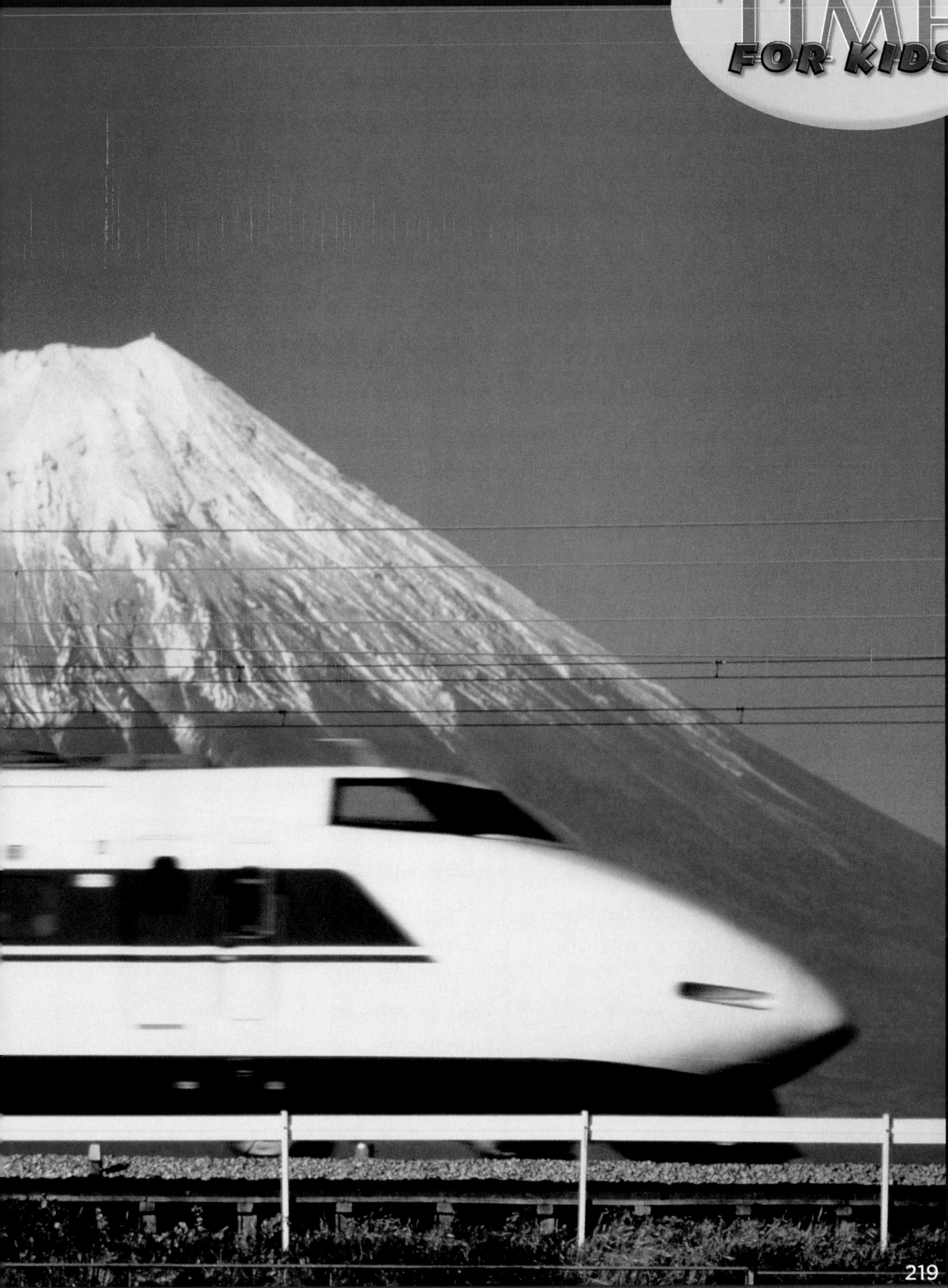

Vocabulary

powered	**artist's**
declared	**pride**
existed	

Visions of the Future from the Past

What opinions did experts have about movement and transportation throughout history? Take a look.

Lord Kelvin, a famous scientist, 1800s

Opinion: Airplanes would never fly.

Was he right? No. On December 17, 1903, the Wright brothers made the first controlled flight in a **powered** airplane.

Lee DeForest, a pioneer in radio, TV, and radar, 1900s

Opinion: No person would ever reach the moon.

Was he right? No. On July 20, 1969, Neil Armstrong stepped onto the moon and **declared**, "That's one small step for man, one giant leap for mankind."

Jules Verne, science-fiction writer, in an 1870 novel

Opinion: People would be able to travel under water in airtight vessels.

Was he right? Yes. Though submarines already **existed**, it would be decades before they could stay submerged for long-distance travel.

Leonardo da Vinci, artist, scientist, inventor, 1400s

Opinion: People would fly in a machine with an overhead propeller.

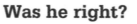

Was he right? Yes. This **artist's** sketch, made about 1490, shows a helicopter 400 years before its invention.

SMOOTH RIDING

This time line of inventions shows some real *movement!*

3800-3600 B.C.	The wheel
1783 A.D.	Hot air balloon
	Steamship
1831	Lawn mower
1885	Bicycle
1903	The Wright brothers' first flight
1908	Ford Model-T car
1939	Jet airplane
1980	In-line skates
1981	Space shuttle

LOG ON Find out more about transportation at
www.macmillanmh.com

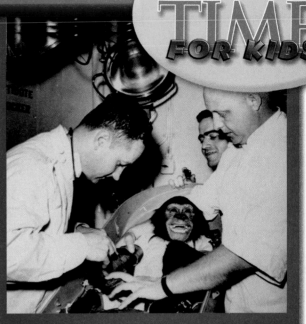

Where No Chimp Has Gone Before

On January 31, 1961, Ham the chimpanzee blasted off into space . . . and history books.

Ham's flight took him 156.5 miles into space at a speed of 5,800 miles per hour. The trip lasted 16.5 minutes. Then Ham's capsule splashed down into the Atlantic Ocean. Back on land, he gobbled up an apple and half an orange.

The U.S. space program took great **pride** in Ham. He paved the way for Alan Shepard to become the first American in space in May 1961.

After his space flight, Ham went on to live in a North Carolina zoo.

Comprehension

Genre

A **Nonfiction Article** gives information about a real person, place, or event.

Make Inferences and Analyze

Fact and Opinion

A fact can be proved to be true. An opinion is a belief that does not have to be supported by facts.

A Carousel of Dreams

The creatures on the Children's Carousel at Riverbank State Park (above) were copied from kids' drawings, like the one below.

The carousel at Riverbank State Park in New York City is probably the most fantastic carousel in the country. It doesn't hold the usual herd of painted ponies. Instead, giant spiders pull a chariot, and a plaid zebra prances beside a two-headed octopus. These creatures were invented by kids. Milo Mottola, 32, is the artist who turned the kids' drawings into carousel critters.

222

Mottola believed kids should be a big part of his carousel project, so he held drawing classes in Riverbank State Park. The kids created more than 1,000 drawings of creatures. It was tough to choose only 32 of them for the carousel. "They were all my favorites!" Mottola **declared**.

When 9-year-old Grover Austin heads to the carousel, he hops on the green lion. He thinks it's the best because he created it! The **artist's** signature is carved on the floor beneath each animal. The original drawing hangs above it.

The Children's Carousel at Riverbank State Park is one of only 200 major carousels that remain today. Amusement parks and fairs now have faster rides. People today seem to prefer rides that are scarier or more exciting than the gentle carousels. But during the early 1900s, carousels were very popular. About 6,000 of them **existed** in the United States.

History in the Round

At one time, carousels were considered rides for adults, not kids. Most carousels were created by craftspeople who came to the U.S. from other countries. They had a lot of **pride** in their designs of fancy horses and chariots. Chariots are the carousel seats that are like benches or little carriages. Most of these old-style carousels are gone. Some were destroyed by fires and other disasters. Many were simply not taken care of. Some originals, however, are still standing and most likely are still making people happy. One of them is in San Diego, California. Another one is in Memphis, Tennessee.

Milo Mottola with some of the carousel's kid artists and their creations

223

The carousel that twirls in Seaport Village, San Diego, was built in 1895. The 41 hand-carved horses have natural horsehair tails. The 13 other animals include a giraffe, a dragon, a teddy bear, an elephant, a camel, a dog, and a lion. They were all made by hand, too. "This is one of the two best carousels in the entire nation," says Brad Perron. He's the owner of a company that fixes old carousels so they are like new again. "They don't make them this way anymore," says Perron. He's talking about animals carved by hand from wood. Newer carousel animals are usually made out of material that is mostly plastic. Some people think the old carousels were better than newer ones.

Riders of the Grand Carousel in Memphis, Tennessee, can choose to ride one of the 48 wooden horses or two hand-carved chariots. Built in 1909, the carousel spun its magic in Chicago, Illinois, for about ten years. Now it is a famous attraction in Tennessee's Libertyland Amusement Park. This carousel is one of a kind. It is so important that it is listed in the National Register of Historic Places.

The Grand Carousel in Memphis, Tennessee

These and other historic carousels are **powered** by a motor in the center of the ride. The motor is covered up by panels with pretty drawings and carvings on them. Older carousels even have mirrors and special music that blares from nearby speakers. Blinking, bright lights call riders to come take a spin.

Did You Know?

* The earliest known carousel in the U.S. appeared in Salem, Massachusetts, in 1799.

* Some historic carousel horses were made with brass rings so that people could try to grab on for a free ride.

* Usually, the fanciest and most decorated horses on a carousel are the ones facing the outside.

* Many original carousel horses built in the early 1900s had real horsehair.

* What's the difference between a carousel and a merry-go-round? Traditionally, carousels had only horses, but merry-go-rounds included other animals.

* Original wooden carousel horses today cost between $200 and $80,000 each.

Think and Compare

1. Brad Perron says that the carousel at Seaport Village in San Diego is "one of the two best carousels in the entire nation." Is that a fact or an opinion? How do you know?

2. How were the creatures on the carousel at Riverbank State Park created?

3. If you could choose to ride a carousel or a faster, scarier ride at an amusement park, which would you choose? Why?

4. Compare the motion of the space capsule that Ham the chimpanzee rode with the motion of a carousel.

225

GETTING A FREE RIDE

Bikes are left for people to use.

Suppose you find a bright yellow bike on a street corner in the city. You hop on and pedal away. But wait—isn't this stealing? No one yells, "Stop! Thief!" That's because this free ride is just fine with the city.

You can find hundreds of free yellow bikes in some U.S. cities. The idea began in Portland, Oregon, in 1994. People saw a need for free transportation, and they wanted to help control pollution. So, to get citizens out of their cars and onto pollution-free bikes, they started the Yellow Bike Project.

The public bikes are painted bright yellow and placed throughout the city. People can hop on a yellow bike and pedal to work, to school, or to run errands. They then leave the bike for the next rider. There have been times when bikes have been stolen, but most people obey the rules. What would be the point of stealing something that's already free?

Portland's idea quickly caught on. Within two years of its start, similar programs were set up in cities in six other states.

Go On ▶

Directions: Answer the questions.

1. Why was the Yellow Bike Project started?

A to teach people who don't have a bike how to ride

B to teach bike safety and rules in cities

C to help control pollution by reducing the use of cars

D to sell more bicycles in cities

2. Which of the following is a FACT about the Yellow Bike Project?

A The bikes cause pollution.

B The idea began in Portland, Oregon.

C People need low-cost transportation.

D Yellow bikes are sold to the public.

3. The photo caption helps explain that

A yellow bike programs are found in many places.

B the bikes are painted bright yellow.

C the idea of free bikes caught on quickly.

D the bikes are left for the next rider.

4. Why is stealing not a problem with the Yellow Bike Project?

5. Why should cities have programs to cut down on air pollution? Give your opinion and list several reasons why you feel this way.

Tip

Form an opinion.

STOP   227

Write to a Prompt

In "A Carousel of Dreams" you read about old and new carousels. Rides such as carousels are entertaining and exciting. Tell about the first time you went on a carousel or another ride. Write a story in three paragraphs describing your experience.

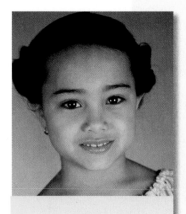

I listed all my ideas before I started writing.

Giddyap, Horsey!

I gave my blue ticket to the man and ran to the horse I had chosen. I climbed up and held the gold pole with both hands. Loud music started, and the carousel began to turn.

My beautiful horse galloped up and down. The purple-gray mane looked like it was waving in the air. My saddle was painted bright red, blue, and yellow. The horse was grayish with smoky black spots. It was the best horse on the carousel!

When the ride stopped, I looked at the other people. A little kid about 2 years old had started to cry. A grandma sat on a bench with a baby on her lap. The baby's eyes were really big! Some big kids looked disappointed that the ride was over. This was my first carousel ride. I rode that same horse three more times that day!

Writing Prompt

In "A Carousel of Dreams" you read that carousels used to be very popular rides. In three paragraphs, write about your favorite ride at an amusement park or a fair. Tell about a time you rode on it, what you liked about it, and why it is your favorite ride. Make sure your story has a beginning, a middle, and an ending.

Writer's Checklist

- ☑ Ask yourself, who will read my story?
- ☑ Think about your purpose for writing.
- ☑ Plan your writing before beginning.
- ☑ Use details to support your story.
- ☑ Be sure your story has a beginning, a middle, and an ending.
- ☑ Use your best spelling, grammar, and punctuation.

Talk About It

A hero is any person who helps others. What qualities do all heroes have?

 LOG ON Find out more about heroes at **www.macmillanmh.com**

HEROES

To the Rescue

by Daniel Dahari

It was recess time. It was a perfect spring day, and Ms. Clark's class hurried outdoors.

Erica headed straight for the slide. There was nothing better than a climb and a slide. Especially on a day like this! She was just about to place her foot on the ladder when she stopped and **screamed** with fear. Everyone ran over to find out what had happened. Erica stood there, **numb**. She couldn't move an inch. Under the ladder's first rung was a turtle, a big turtle—and it was stuck!

"Stand clear," warned Ms. Clark. "It's trying to **escape**, but it can't get out. Poor thing."

Several boys and girls **fled** across the yard. That turtle looked mean.

"That's a snapping turtle," said Jeff. "Snappers have really strong jaws. That thing can really bite! I wonder how it got here."

The turtle tried to dig with its feet but remained stuck.

"I'll call the police," said Ms. Clark. "They'll send over Animal Control. They'll know what to do."

An Animal Control van pulled up and **shuddered** to a stop. The officer said, "That's a snapping turtle, all right. It must have come up from the marsh. We'd better get him back where he belongs."

She got a small shovel and carefully removed the sand beneath the turtle. Then the officer gently wrapped the turtle in a towel. She said, "You did the right thing by calling me. It's very dangerous to try to free a trapped animal yourselves."

Ms. Clark took a picture. "This **image** will go on the front page of the school **newspaper** next week," she said. "It's not every day that we get a snapshot of a snapping turtle!"

Reread for **Comprehension**

Make Inferences and Analyze
Make and Confirm Predictions
When you make predictions, you are making an inference about what you think might happen in the story based on the story clues.

A Predictions Chart can help you analyze clues to make good predictions. Reread the story to confirm what you predicted.

What I Predict	What Happens

Comprehension

Genre

Realistic Fiction is an invented story that could have happened in real life.

Make Inferences and Analyze

Make and Confirm Predictions

As you read, use your Predictions Chart.

What I Predict	What Happens

Read to Find Out

Will the printer become friends with everyone at the plant?

THE PRINTER

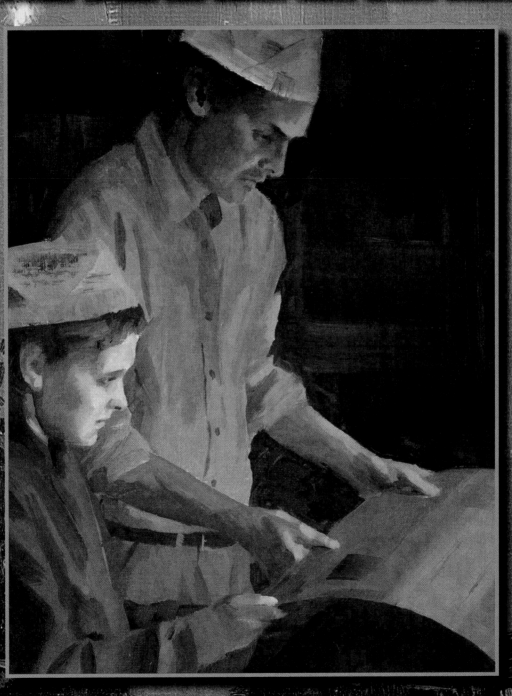

by Myron Uhlberg
illustrated by Henri Sørensen

My father was a printer. He wore a printer's four-cornered **newspaper** hat. Every day after work, he brought home the next day's paper. After reading it, he always folded a page into a small hat and gently placed it on my head.

I would not take off my newspaper hat until bedtime.

My father was deaf. Though he could not hear, he felt through the soles of his shoes the pounding and rumbling of the giant printing presses that daily spat out the newspaper he helped create.

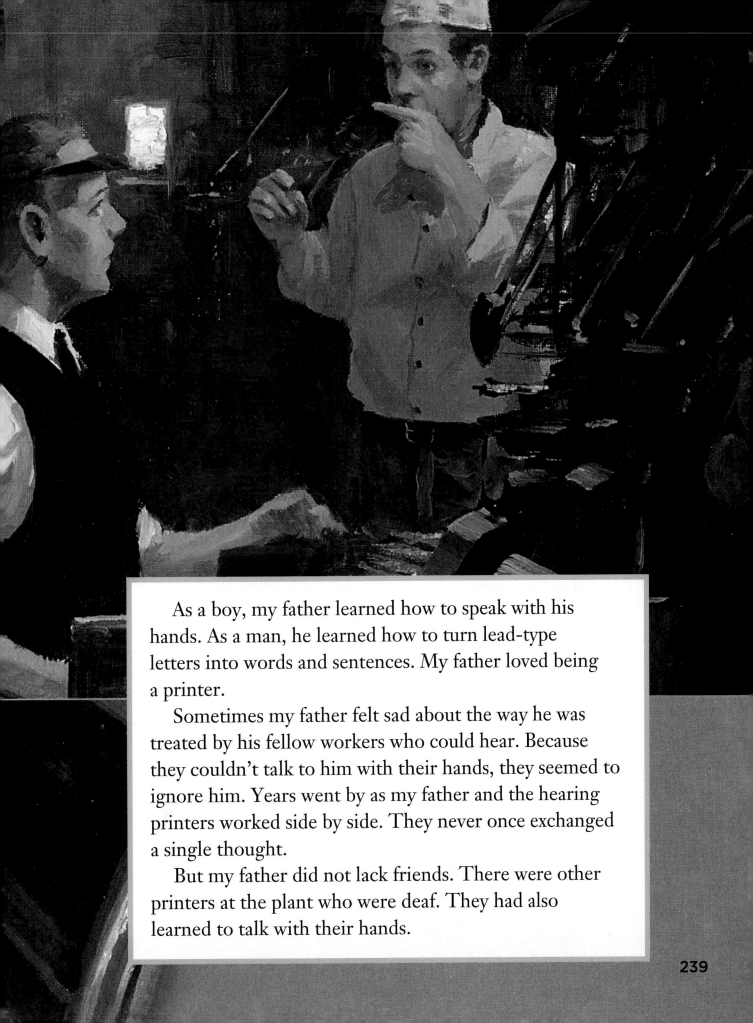

As a boy, my father learned how to speak with his hands. As a man, he learned how to turn lead-type letters into words and sentences. My father loved being a printer.

Sometimes my father felt sad about the way he was treated by his fellow workers who could hear. Because they couldn't talk to him with their hands, they seemed to ignore him. Years went by as my father and the hearing printers worked side by side. They never once exchanged a single thought.

But my father did not lack friends. There were other printers at the plant who were deaf. They had also learned to talk with their hands.

One day, while the giant presses ran, their noises shutting out all other sound, my father spotted a fire flickering in a far corner of the pressroom.

The fire was spreading quickly, silently. Suddenly, the wood floor burst into flames.

My father knew he had to tell everyone. He couldn't speak to shout a warning. Even if he could, no one would hear him over the loud roar of the presses.

But he could speak with his hands.

Make and Confirm Predictions
How will the printer tell people about the fire?

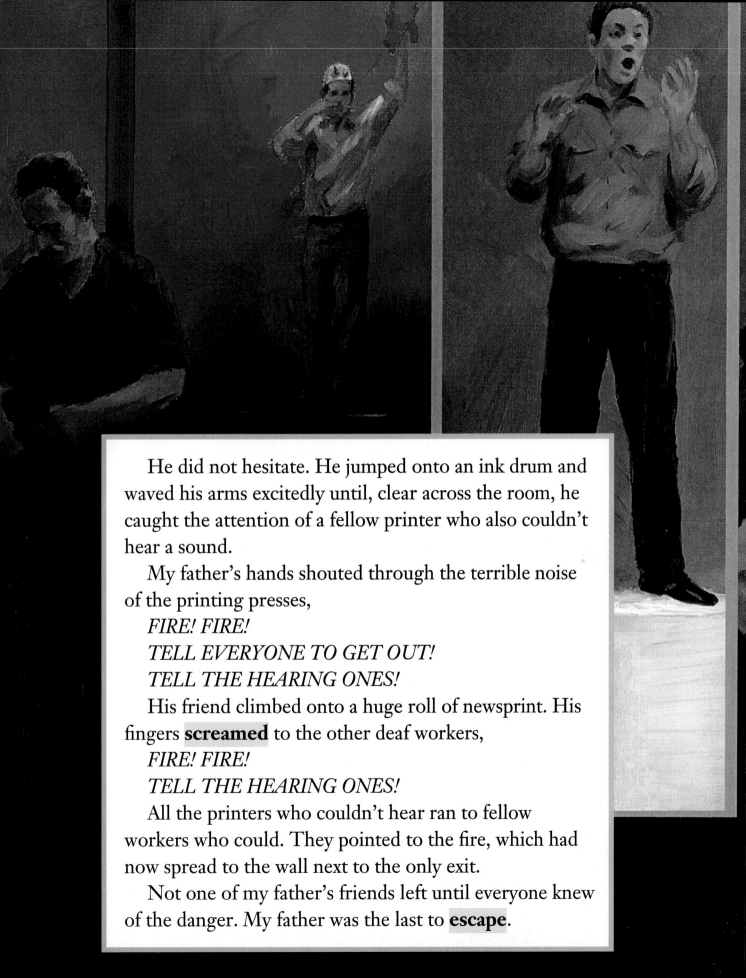

He did not hesitate. He jumped onto an ink drum and waved his arms excitedly until, clear across the room, he caught the attention of a fellow printer who also couldn't hear a sound.

My father's hands shouted through the terrible noise of the printing presses,
FIRE! FIRE!
TELL EVERYONE TO GET OUT!
TELL THE HEARING ONES!

His friend climbed onto a huge roll of newsprint. His fingers **screamed** to the other deaf workers,
FIRE! FIRE!
TELL THE HEARING ONES!

All the printers who couldn't hear ran to fellow workers who could. They pointed to the fire, which had now spread to the wall next to the only exit.

Not one of my father's friends left until everyone knew of the danger. My father was the last to **escape**.

By the time everyone had **fled**, the fire—feeding on huge quantities of paper—had engulfed the enormous plant. The giant presses, some still spewing out burning sheets of newspaper, had fallen partly through the floor. Great shafts of flame shot out of the bursting windows.

The printers stood in the street, broken glass at their feet. They embraced one another as the fire engines arrived. They were happy to be alive.

My father stood alone, struck **numb** by the last **image** of the burning presses.

The fire destroyed the printing presses. The plant had to close for repairs. But not one printer had been hurt.

When the printing plant finally reopened, my father went back to the work he loved. The new presses were switched on and roared into life.

STRATEGY SKILL

Make and Confirm Predictions
How will the hearing printers treat the narrator's father now that the plant has reopened?

When the day's newspaper had been printed, the presses **shuddered** to a stop. Now there was silence.

In the midst of the stillness, my father's co-workers gathered around him. They presented him with a hat made of the freshly printed newspaper.

And as my father put the hat on his head, all the printers who could hear did something surprising.

They told him THANK YOU with their hands.

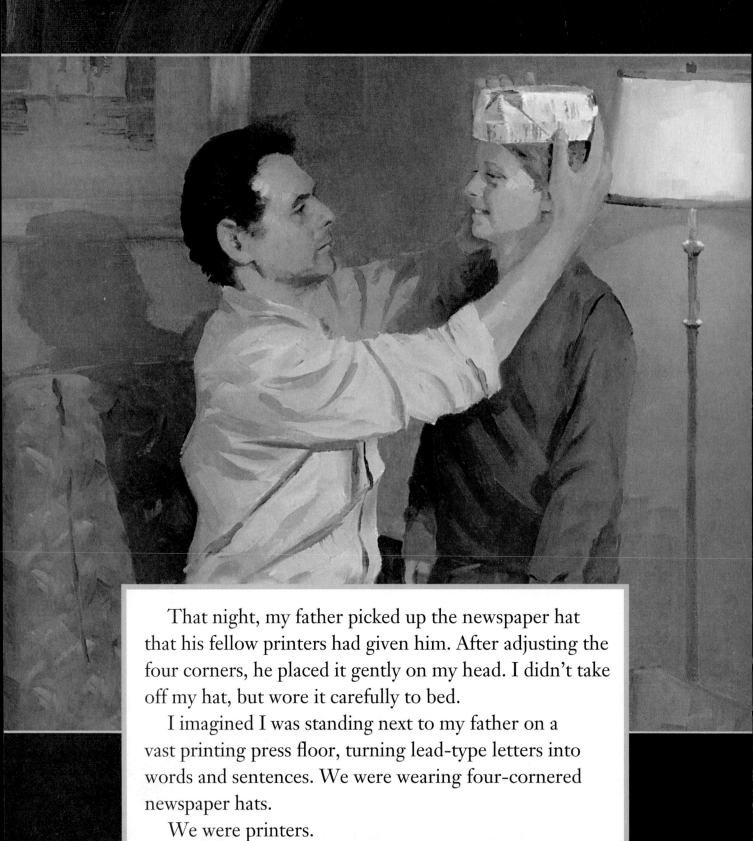

That night, my father picked up the newspaper hat that his fellow printers had given him. After adjusting the four corners, he placed it gently on my head. I didn't take off my hat, but wore it carefully to bed.

I imagined I was standing next to my father on a vast printing press floor, turning lead-type letters into words and sentences. We were wearing four-cornered newspaper hats.

We were printers.

SAVE THE DAY WITH MYRON AND HENRI

Author

Myron Uhlberg used memories of his father to write his story. Myron's father was born deaf. He worked as a newspaper printer just like the father in the story. When Myron was young, he would visit his father at work. Even today, Myron still remembers how noisy the pressroom was. He also remembers the hats his father made out of newspaper for him.

Other books by Myron Uhlberg: *Flying Over Brooklyn* and *Mad Dog McGraw*

Illustrator

Henri Sørensen grew up in Denmark and spent much of his childhood in a quiet museum. Every week he visited the museum to look at paintings. When Henri illustrates a story, he thinks about how the words make him feel. Then he tries to show the feeling in his pictures.

 Find out more about Myron Uhlberg and Henri Sørensen at **www.macmillanmh.com**

Author's Purpose

Did Myron Uhlberg write to persuade or entertain readers? Explain. Use details from *The Printer* to support your answer.

Comprehension Check

Summarize

Use the Predictions Chart to help you summarize what happens in *The Printer*. Tell what you thought would happen and what really happened at the end of the story.

What I Predict	What Happens

Think and Compare

1. When the deaf printer noticed the fire in the **newspaper** plant, what did you predict would happen next? Were you right? Explain. **Make Inferences and Analyze: Make and Confirm Predictions**

2. Reread page 248. What is the importance of the hearing printers learning how to say "thank you" in sign language? **Evaluate**

3. If you did not know sign language, how would you tell a friend who is deaf something important? Explain. **Synthesize**

4. Before the fire, the hearing printers seemed to ignore the deaf printer. Why? **Analyze**

5. Read "To the Rescue" on pages 232-233. How are the warning and rescue in this story different from the warning and rescue in *The Printer?* Use details from both selections in your answer. **Reading/Writing Across Texts**

Social Studies

Genre

Nonfiction Articles give information about real people, places, or things.

Text Feature

A **Map** is a drawing that shows the surface features of an area.

Content Vocabulary

remote

smokejumpers

physical

retreat

Smokejumpers

by Roland Hosein

Some wildfires start in places so **remote** that there are no roads or open spaces for a helicopter to land. When this happens, it is time to call in the **smokejumpers**. They are firefighters trained to parachute close to remote wildfires and put them out.

Smokejumpers need to move fast. They need to get to fires while they are still small.

There are nine smokejumper bases in the United States. One of these is in California. During the summer, the danger of fire in California can be very high. The map below shows the fire danger in different parts of the state. Let's take a look at what it's like to be a smokejumper in California.

Smokejumper Training

It takes six and a half weeks of training to become a California smokejumper. Only those with experience fighting fires in the wild are chosen for this training.

California Fire Danger

Reading a Map

This map uses different colors to show the fire danger levels in different parts of the state.

MAP KEY

Moderate
High
Very High
Water

The map key shows what the colors mean.

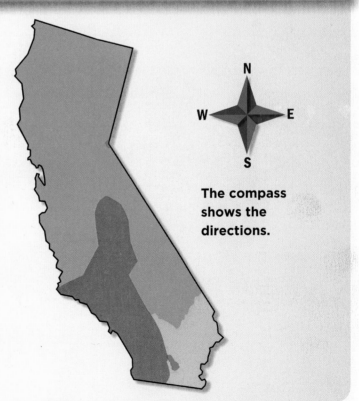

The compass shows the directions.

It takes a great deal of **physical**, or body, strength to be a smokejumper. Much time is spent stretching, running, and carrying heavy gear. All smokejumpers must be able to parachute from a plane, steer around trees, and climb at least 150 feet up a tree with all their equipment.

The Fire Call

As soon as a request for help comes in, the smokejumpers move quickly. They put on padded jump jackets and pants. They also wear a helmet with a wire-mesh face mask. Each jumper carries a small gear bag. It contains water, fire shelter, a hard hat, and gloves. They need to be on the plane within 10 minutes.

After the jumpers have landed, firefighting gear is dropped from the plane. The crew leader decides on a safe spot where the smokejumpers can **retreat**, or move back to, if the fire comes too close. Once this spot is chosen, it's time to fight the fire!

First, the smokejumpers clear around the edge of the fire to keep it from spreading. Then they might radio for water or chemicals to be dropped onto the blaze. When the fire is under control, the smokejumpers put it out with water. Before they leave, smokejumpers make sure that the whole area is completely cool.

After they finish putting out a fire, smokejumpers are often picked up by a helicopter, but sometimes they must hike out to the nearest road while carrying all their tools and gear!

Once they return to their base, they rest … until the next fire call comes in.

Connect and Compare

1. Look at the map on page 255. What is the fire danger level for most of California? How can you tell? **Reading a Map**

2. What are some personality traits that smokejumpers are likely to have? **Analyze**

3. How is the boy's father in *The Printer* like the smokejumpers you just read about? How is he different? **Reading/Writing Across Texts**

Social Studies Activity

Use the library to do research on firefighters. Find out what kind of special clothing and equipment they use. Draw a firefighter wearing the equipment. Label and explain what each piece is for.

 LOG ON Find out more about firefighters at **www.macmillanmh.com**

Write an Introductory Speech

I included personal opinions to tell how I feel about the best teacher in school.

I included facts about Mrs. Adorno's extra efforts.

Meet Mrs. Adorno

by Edward M.

Today we are giving the award for favorite teacher to Mrs. Adorno. She is the nicest, funniest teacher I have ever had. A lot of you must think so too, because you voted for her. Mrs. Adorno is the only person who can make science seem like fun. After school she meets with students who need extra help. Mrs. Adorno always makes us laugh, and she is our softball team's biggest fan. In addition, she designed our new softball uniforms. Now say hello to our favorite teacher, Mrs. Adorno!

Your Turn

Pretend that someone is getting an award and you have to give a speech to introduce that person. It might be a famous person or someone you know. Write your speech in one paragraph. Be sure to describe this person and include both facts and opinions. Use the Writer's Checklist to check your writing.

Writer's Checklist

✓ **Ideas and Content:** Have I clearly explained why this person is receiving an award?

✓ **Organization:** Did I include a topic sentence?

☐ **Voice:** Do my **opinions** show enthusiasm?

✓ **Word Choice:** Did I choose words that describe the person and show how I feel?

✓ **Sentence Fluency:** Does my speech flow smoothly when I read it out loud?

✓ **Conventions:** Did I make sure that pronouns and verbs agree? Did I check my spelling?

ANIMAL ARCHITECTS

261

Web Spinners

by Steven Kutner

Vocabulary

hives	retreats
architects	shallow
structures	shelter
contain	

Analogies

An **analogy** shows how two pairs of words are alike. The analogy below compares the homes of two animals.

bee is to *hive* as *spider* is to *web*

Just as bees build **hives** to live in, spiders spin webs. Spiders are talented **architects**. They design and build **structures** to live in that are works of art. These structures are also traps for other insects.

Spinning Silk

Spider webs are made from silk. Spiders make silk in their bellies. Their silk-making gland has many tiny holes. The silk goes through the holes to get outside the spider's body. When it meets the air, the silk forms a thread. The thread is very thin but very strong.

Spiders can make different kinds of silk. Some **contain** a material that makes the silk sticky. Other silks do not have this material.

A spider spins a thread behind itself everywhere it goes. This thread is called a dragline. If an enemy comes near, the spider **retreats** on its dragline. Being able to go backwards on its own line is like having a self-made escape route!

Tangled Webs

Different spiders build different kinds of webs. The simplest web is called a tangled web. It is just a mess of threads that are attached to something. A cobweb is a dusty, old, tangled web.

Cellar Spiders

Some spiders are called cellar spiders. This is because they usually build tangled webs in cellars or other dark places.

Orb Weavers

The most common webs are shaped like wheels. They are built by orb weavers. You can find these webs in open areas, such as the spaces between branches.

Water Spiders

The water spider builds its web in tiny ponds and other places with **shallow** water. The web looks like a small air-filled balloon. The water spider feeds and raises its family inside this cozy **shelter**.

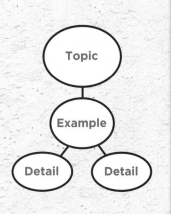

Reread for **Comprehension**

Summarize
Description

In an article an author will describe each part of a topic to organize information. Use the description of each part of the topic to summarize what you have read.

A Description Web helps you remember details so that you can summarize the topic. Reread "Web Spinners" and record the details of one description.

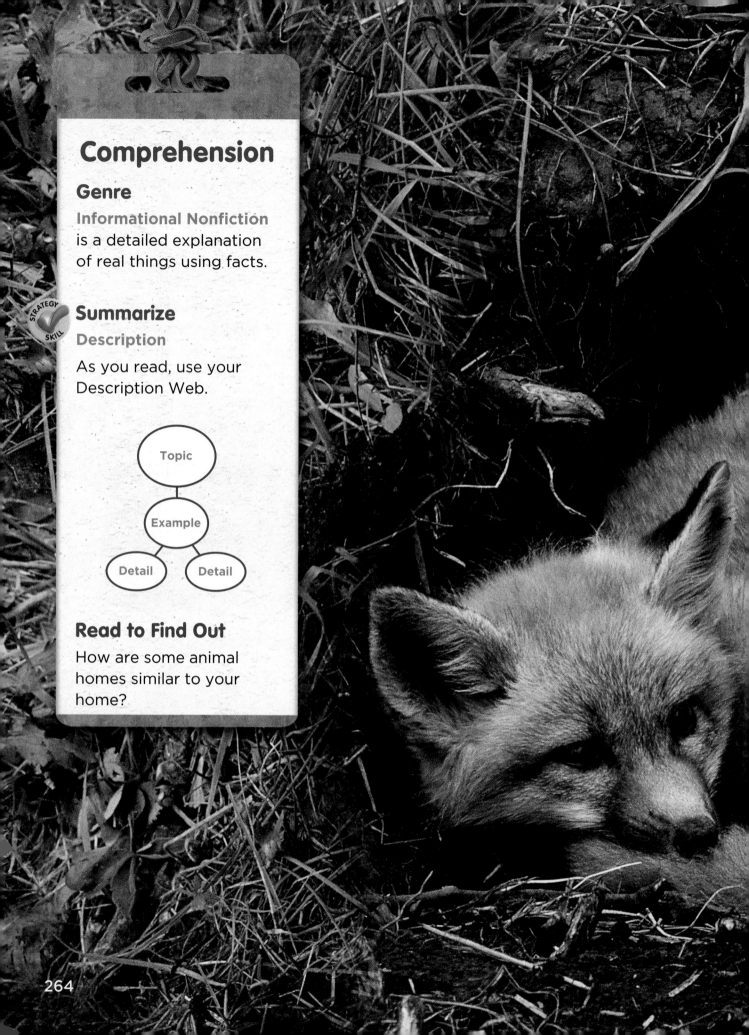

Comprehension

Genre

Informational Nonfiction is a detailed explanation of real things using facts.

Summarize

Description

As you read, use your Description Web.

Topic

Example

Detail   Detail

Read to Find Out

How are some animal homes similar to your home?

Animal Homes

by Ann O. Squire

Why Do Animals Need Homes?

Animals need homes for many of the same reasons that people do. What are some of those reasons? Start by thinking about your own home, and the kinds of things you do there.

Some kinds of penguins build nests to protect their chicks.

Eating is one very important thing you do every day. Your house has a kitchen where you store and prepare food. Some animals also keep food in their homes. Honeybees, for example, live in **hives** made up of waxy honeycombs. Each honeycomb has many six-sided cubbies, or cells, where the bees store their honey.

The cells of the honeycomb are also used as nurseries for young bees. And that may remind you of another reason people and animals need homes. They need a safe place to raise their young. Birds' nests, alligator mounds, and the dens of polar bears are other kinds of homes made for raising a family.

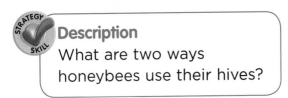

Description

What are two ways honeybees use their hives?

▲ **Other cells are used as nurseries for bee larvae.**

Bees store honey in some ▶ of the cells of their hive.

A desert tortoise in its burrow

Doesn't it feel good to come indoors on a cold winter day or turn up the air conditioner on a hot and humid summer night? That's another reason we need a home—to protect us from bad weather.

The desert tortoise lives in dry parts of the southwestern United States, where summer temperatures often go above 100 degrees Fahrenheit (38 degrees Celsius). To escape the heat, the tortoise digs a **shallow** burrow, or hole, where it can rest during the hottest part of the day.

In the winter, when temperatures fall below freezing, the tortoise digs a much deeper burrow. Then it climbs in and spends the winter there, hibernating with other tortoises.

Underground burrows also give animals a place to hide from their enemies. Prairie dogs, for example, dig long, winding burrows with many different rooms and tunnels.

Many people's homes have a front door, a back door and maybe even a side door. A prairie-dog burrow has several openings, too. If a hungry predator invades the burrow through the main entrance, the prairie dogs can escape out the back way.

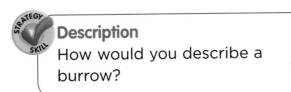

STRATEGY SKILL

Description
How would you describe a burrow?

A prairie dog standing near its burrow entrance

A coyote trying to invade a prairie-dog burrow

Some animals build homes for more tricky reasons. Many spiders spin webs mainly to trap unlucky insects.

Now that you know some of the reasons animals need homes, let's find out about some unusual animal homes.

A weaverbird
building its nest

Building a Home

Many animals build their own homes. These animal **architects** can be birds, mammals, insects, and even fish.

The African weaverbird's name is a clue to the way this bird builds its nest. The male weaverbird gathers long blades of grass, which he knots and weaves into a sturdy ring. Then he adds grass to the ring, making a hollow ball. To keep out tree snakes, the ball is open only at the bottom. When the nest is finished, the weaverbird calls to attract nearby females. If a female likes the nest, she moves in, and the two raise a family.

◀ **A spider trapping prey in its web**

Termite towers have many rooms.

Some insects build homes, too. One of the largest and most complicated **structures** in the animal world is created by tiny African termites.

A termite tower may be as tall as a giraffe and **contain** millions of termites. The walls of the tower are made of a rock-hard mixture of dirt and saliva. They contain air shafts that keep the inside of the tower cool, even in the blazing sun.

The tower has many special rooms. It has a royal chamber, where the termite king and queen live, nurseries for the young, rooms for storing food, and even an underground garden. Most termites live for only a few years, but a termite tower may last for close to a century.

A termite tower in Ghana, Africa

Beavers use sticks and mud to build a dam. Then they build their lodge in the middle of the pond formed by the dam.

Have you ever heard people say someone is as "busy as a beaver"? You'd know what they mean if you saw how much work goes into building a beaver lodge.

First, the beavers use sticks and mud to make a dam across a stream. Then water backs up behind the dam to form a pond. In the center of the pond, the beavers build their lodge. It looks like nothing more than a pile of sticks, but the lodge has a room inside that is reached by underwater tunnels. The beavers can come and go easily, but it's almost impossible for wolves and other predators to find a way in.

The hermit crab makes its home in an empty seashell.

Finding a Home

Bees, weaverbirds, termites, and beavers all work long and hard to build their homes. But some animals take the easy way out. They look around for ready-made lodgings.

Unlike most other crabs, the hermit crab does not have a hard shell to protect it. It needs a safe place to live, so the hermit crab searches for an empty snail shell. When it finds a shell that fits, the hermit crab squeezes inside. It stays there until it grows too big for that shell. Then it must look for a larger shell.

The pea crab doesn't even wait until a shell is empty. This tiny crab moves in with the original owner! It squeezes into the shell of a mussel, clam, or oyster while that animal is still alive. The shellfish isn't even bothered by the pea crab sharing its home. As the shellfish filters food through its gills, the pea crab catches tiny bits of food as they float past.

A pea crab

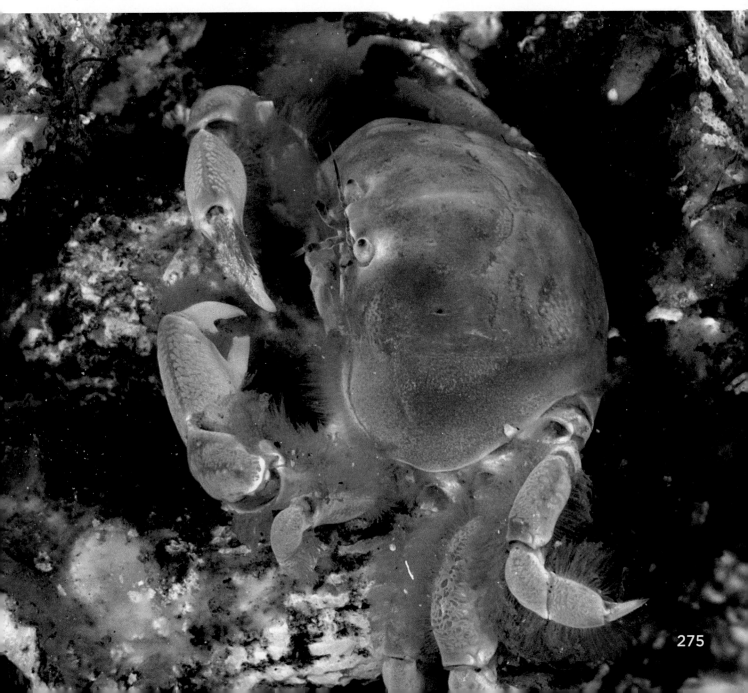

A white cowbird egg in a nest containing blue wood thrush eggs

A cowbird chick being raised by a yellow warbler

The cowbird is even more daring. Instead of building its own nest, the female cowbird searches the forest for other nesting birds. When she sees a likely couple, she settles down to wait.

As soon as the unsuspecting birds leave their nest, the cowbird darts in and throws out one of their eggs. Then she quickly lays one of her own. The nesting birds never know the difference! They raise the cowbird chick as if it were one of their own.

Burrowing owls ▶

Birds don't usually live underground, but one that does is the burrowing owl. These long-legged owls sometimes move into abandoned prairie-dog burrows. The birds come out in the cool of the evening to hunt small rodents, frogs, and insects.

Mobile Homes

A turtle can protect itself by retreating into its shell.

Most people and most animals live in homes that stay in one place. But if you've ever traveled in a camper, trailer or boat, you know that some kinds of homes can move around with you. Did you know that some animals also live in "mobile homes"?

Tortoises and turtles move slowly. You might think they would be easy prey for any animal that wanted to eat them. But tortoises and turtles can escape into the safety of their homes in a flash, simply by pulling their head and feet inside their hard shell.

Turtles sunning themselves
on a log

The snail is another animal that carries its house on its back. Snails need damp conditions in order to survive. In cold or dry weather, the snail **retreats** into its spiral shell to avoid drying out.

Like turtles, snails can retreat into their shells.

A kind of caterpillar called the bagworm makes its home out of twigs woven together with silk. The bagworm lives inside this silken case and drags its **shelter** along as it moves from branch to branch feeding on leaves.

A bagworm hanging from a spruce tree

279

At Home with Ann

AUTHOR
Ann O. Squire

is an expert on how animals behave. Before Ann began to write books for children, she studied many different kinds of animals. She has studied everything from rats to the African electric fish.

Other books by Ann O. Squire: *Growing Crystals* and *Seashells*

LOG ON Find out more about Ann O. Squire at **www.macmillanmh.com**

Author's Purpose

Nonfiction authors often write to inform or persuade. Why did Ann O. Squire write *Animal Homes*? What are some details that help you understand her purpose?

Comprehension Check

Summarize

Use the Description Web to help you summarize facts about *Animal Homes.* Create a topic sentence about animal homes, and then describe important information about different kinds of animal homes.

Topic

Example

Detail   Detail

Think and Compare

1. Choose an animal that carries its **shelter** around. Using details from the text and your Description Web, describe that animal and its home. **Summarize: Description**

2. Reread pages 278-279 of *Animal Homes.* What do you think is the most useful thing about having a mobile home? **Analyze**

3. Which animal home in this story would you choose to see in person? Explain your answer. **Synthesize**

4. Is it important for people to learn about animal homes? Why or why not? **Evaluate**

5. Read "Web Spinners" on pages 262-263. Look at the photographs in the two selections you have read. Compare the structures of the spider webs to the structure of another animal home. Use details from both selections in your answer. **Reading/Writing Across Texts**

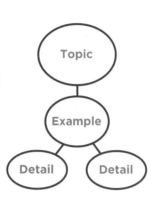

Home Sweet Home

Poetry

A **Limerick** is a short funny poem. It has five lines. Usually the last words in the first, second, and fifth lines rhyme. The third and fourth lines usually rhyme with each other.

SKILL

Literary Elements

A **Simile** compares two different things by using the words *like* or *as*.

A **Rhythmic Pattern** is a series of stressed and unstressed syllables that create a beat.

A flea on a pooch doesn't care
Which part it is crossing to where.
    Like mud to a frog
    Any part of a dog
Suits a flea, and it's glad to be there.

— *John Ciardi*

The rhythmic pattern of these two lines creates the beat: da DAH da da DAH da da DAH.

282

Limerick

Think of darkness. Then think of the mole

In his tunnel: black, black as coal.

But the traffic is light,

And the weather's all right,

And the tunnel is free—there's no toll.

— *David McCord*

This simile compares two unlike things; the darkness of the tunnel and coal.

Connect and Compare

1. In the second limerick, what picture comes to mind when you read the simile "black as coal"? **Simile**

2. Reread the first two lines of "Home Sweet Home." Do these two lines have the same rhythmic pattern? **Evaluate**

3. Do the mole and the flea both like their homes? Explain your answer. **Reading/Writing Across Texts**

LOG ON Find out more about limericks at **www.macmillanmh.com**

283

Write a Descriptive Poem

Writer's Craft

Figurative Language

Poetry paints pictures with words. Use **figurative language**, such as similes, in poems. Similes compare two things that are not alike. Similes use *like* or *as*.

Turtles Don't Hurry

by Sam C.

I wrote a simile to compare lizards to rabbits.

I used descriptive words to describe how a turtle moves.

Turtles are reptiles,
As everyone knows.
They're cold-blooded,
And they have feet and tiny toes.
While lizards are quick,
Like rabbits with scales,
Turtles don't hurry.
They move slow like snails.
They'll never leap up,
Or jump out or attack.
You'd move slowly, too,
With a house on your back!

Your Turn

Write a descriptive poem that is about six to ten lines long. Your poem could be about any animal that makes its own home. Use figurative language that creates a "picture" for the reader. Use the Writer's Checklist to check your writing.

Writer's Checklist

☑ **Ideas and Content:** Did I use **figurative language** that paints a picture?

☑ **Organization:** Is my writing structured like a poem rather than a paragraph?

☑ **Voice:** Does my personality come through?

☑ **Word Choice:** Will the precise words of my poem interest my reader?

☑ **Sentence Fluency:** Does my poem make sense?

☑ **Conventions:** Did I use pronoun contractions such as *I've* and *he's* correctly? Did I check my spelling?

Test Strategy

Think and Search

Read on to find the answer. Look for clues in more than one place.

Twister

Swirling, whirling,
and spinning
like a top.
Roaring
like a
train.
When
will it
S
T
O
P
?

—Maryann Dobeck

TORNADOES: NATURE'S TOUGHEST STORMS

What Is a Tornado?

A tornado is a funnel of wind spinning very fast. Its wind can blow as fast as 300 miles per hour, which is almost six times the speed limit on a highway! Tornadoes can be caused by powerful thunderstorms called *supercells*. Cold, dry air mixing with warm, moist air makes a supercell. When the warm air in the supercell rises very quickly, it starts to spin into a tornado.

Tornadoes come in different shapes and sizes.

When a tornado reaches the ground, it begins to travel. The path of a tornado can be straight, zigzag, or circular. The damage along this path can be as wide as one or two miles and as long as 50 miles. Tornadoes typically touch down for only two or three minutes.

At first, a tornado's long cone shape is almost invisible. As it picks up dirt and other materials, the tornado becomes easier to see. A tornado can even pick up cars, trees, and parts of buildings.

The Dangers of Tornadoes

Tornadoes can be very dangerous. The Fujita Pearson Tornado Scale rates the power of tornadoes. Here's how it rates them:

F-0: Wind speed of 40–72 miles per hour. It can break tree branches and damage chimneys.

F-1: Wind speed of 73–112 miles per hour. It can damage roofs and overturn mobile homes.

F-2: Wind speed of 113–157 miles per hour. It can pick up trees and damage houses.

F-3: Wind speed of 158–205 miles per hour. It can destroy house roofs and walls, move cars, and overturn trains.

F-4: Wind speed of 207–260 miles per hour. It can knock down even strong walls in big buildings.

F-5: Wind speed of 261–318 miles per hour. It can lift up and carry houses. It can knock down anything in its path.

Staying Safe in a Tornado

Tornadoes are hard to predict. The sky might appear slightly greenish just before a tornado. Loud winds that sound like a train or an airplane might mean a tornado is very close.

Powerful tornadoes can turn sturdy homes to pieces.

The best place to take cover from a tornado is in a place without windows, such as a cellar, bathroom, hallway, or closet. People in cars should stop driving and get into a building as soon as possible.

Go On ▶

Tip

Look for information.

Directions: Answer the questions.

1. **According to the poem and the article, why is a tornado called a twister?**

   A   It twists things in its path.
   B   The wind spins around.
   C   It is like a puzzle.
   D   It is unpredictable.

2. **What is the relationship between wind speed and a tornado's power?**

   A   Wind speed doesn't matter.
   B   The slowest wind speed does the most damage.
   C   The greatest wind speed does the most damage.
   D   The greatest wind speed does the least damage.

3. **What do you think is the BEST thing to do if a tornado is nearby?**

   A   Get in a car and drive away from the tornado.
   B   Go to the top floor of the building.
   C   Go to a room that has no windows.
   D   Decide which path the tornado is taking.

4. **What causes a tornado to form?**

5. **The thunder is loud, and the sky looks green. What should you do? Use details from the selection in your answer.**

   Writing Prompt
   Some people get close enough to tornadoes
   to take photos and videos. Do you think this
   is a good idea? Write a two-paragraph speech
   explaining your point of view.

STOP

Helping Our Neighbors

Talk About It

We are all neighbors in our hometowns. Why is it good to help our neighbors?

Find out more about helping neighbors at **www.macmillanmh.com**

Vocabulary

downtown	**construction**
appliances	**equipment**
owners	**leaky**

Context Clues

Paragraph Clues can help you figure out the meaning of a word you don't know.

Use clues in the third paragraph to find out what the word *appliances* means.

What Should I Be?

by Carol R.

When I walk around my neighborhood, I see people working to protect and help me and my family. Firefighters, letter carriers, and police officers are community workers. They make my neighborhood a better place to live. When I am older, I would like to be a community worker, but which job should I choose?

Letter Carriers

Letter carriers deliver our mail and drop off packages and magazines. They work in every town and city in the United States.

The letter carrier in my neighborhood is Mr. Vasquez. He works **downtown**, walking from block to block to deliver mail to each address along the route. He doesn't carry big boxes, like the ones that hold stoves and washing machines. Trucks deliver **appliances** like those! Maybe I will be a letter carrier.

Police Officers

Police officers, like Officer Morena, keep us safe. Home and business **owners** depend on the police to guard our families, our property, and our streets.

Police may also work at sites where the **construction** of new buildings takes place. They direct traffic to keep the workers and drivers safe. Officer Morena can find lost people and help if there is an accident. She has special **equipment**, such as a two-way radio, so she can talk to other officers. Being a police officer might be a good job.

Firefighters

Firefighters are brave, like Chief Cole. They risk their lives to save people caught in fires. They also check smoke alarms in schools, as well as fire hydrants along the road to make sure they are tightly sealed. **Leaky** hydrants may not have enough water when the time comes to fight a fire.

Chief Cole is a good firefighter. Maybe I will be one too, someday.

Reread for **Comprehension**

Analyze Story Structure

Theme

When you analyze story structure, you think about how the story is organized. Every story is structured around a theme. The theme of a selection is the message the author wants to get across to the reader.

A Theme Map helps you identify clues to the story's theme using the characters, setting, and plot. Reread the selection to find the theme.

Clue
↓
Clue
↓
Clue
↓
Theme

Comprehension

Genre

Realistic Fiction is an invented story that could have happened in real life.

Analyze Story Structure

Theme

As you read, use your Theme Map.

```
Clue
  ↓
Clue
  ↓
Clue
  ↓
Theme
```

Read to Find Out

What is the theme of this story?

A Castle on Viola Street

by DyAnne DiSalvo

Award Winning Author

In the old days, before I was ten, we rented an apartment on Emerald Street. It was a small place to live in for one whole family, but somehow we made the room.

There always seemed to be enough to go around, even with five people at our table.

Every morning my father would get up even before the sun. "Someday things will change around here," he would whisper to me. He usually said this during the winter when the house was beginning to feel chilly. Then he'd kiss us good-bye, tuck up our blankets, and leave for his job at the diner.

My mother worked part-time in the **downtown** bakery while my sisters and I were at school. After school she'd sit on the stoop and watch us play.

Sometimes my mother would flip through a magazine. She'd show me pictures of houses with gardens and porches. They all looked like castles to me. I'd puff out my cheeks when I looked at our place. It was old and peeling and sorry.

That's when my mother would hug me and say, "Our family is rich in more ways than we can count."

Theme
Why does the mother look at pictures of houses?

On Saturday mornings my mother would weigh my pockets down with quarters for the Laundromat.

"Hold Andy's hand," she'd tell my sister.

Then my mother would slip two brown-bagged lunches in the wagon with a dollar for a treat. My sister and I would bump our cart to the Soap & Go on Viola Street.

298

Now, across the street from the Soap & Go were three boarded-up houses. My father said it was a shame. "Somebody should do something about that," he'd say whenever he saw them. So when a truck pulled up and workers unloaded **equipment**, I started to pay attention.

"What's going on over there?" a lady at the Soap &
Go asked.

Mr. Rivera pointed to a flier that was posted up front.

"I'll bet it has something to do with this," he told
her. The flier had a picture of a house and said
YOU TOO CAN OWN A HOME.

After our laundry was dried and folded, I took my sister by
the hand and rushed our wagon back to Emerald Street.

At supper I told my parents all about what I had heard and seen. My father scrambled eggs with extra zest, and my mother put ice in our water.

"There's a meeting tonight," I said. "Seven o'clock at the school."

Later on, when my parents came home, they were just as excited as I was.

"This organization buys empty houses and fixes them up like new!" said my mother.

"And if you're interested in helping to fix up a house for other people," my father continued, "then one day other people will help fix up a house for you."

That sounded like a good plan to me. It would be nice to live in a house that wasn't so chilly in winter.

"So we signed up," my father told me. "Can we count on you to help?"

I hugged them so tight I almost fell out of bed. I think they knew my answer.

Well, you know how sometimes, when you never believe that anything will ever be different, then one morning you just wake up and nothing is the same? That's what happened to our family that spring when the project on Viola Street began.

Clang! Bang! Bang! Smash! Those workers started early.

"Take a good look," my mother told us. "That's what we'll be doing soon."

"Are all those people getting a house?" I asked.

"Some of them will," my mother said. "But anyone who wants to can help. It's called volunteering."

Piece by piece, the inside of the first house came apart—one old bathtub, some cabinets, sinks. Slats of wood and piping piled up like a mountain full of junk in the Dumpster.

Most people on the block were happy about the project, but other people were not. The lady next door said, "No banging before nine o'clock!" Some people laughed and said out loud, "Who would want a house in a neighborhood like this?"

But my father would smile and whisper to me, "Sometimes new things are hard to get used to and people are slow to change."

On the weekends, when our family showed up, a leader called out the assignments.

"Everyone here will have a special job to do," she said.

My mother scraped wallpaper off crusty walls that
crumbled like toast. My father and I worked together.
He lifted up old linoleum tiles by sliding a cat-hammer
underneath. My job was to carefully hammer down nails on
the floorboards when he was through.

Some volunteers, like us, hoped to have a house
one day.

"We're looking forward to living in a place without
broken windows and **leaky** pipes," Mr. and Mrs. Rivera said.

My father said he couldn't wait to have a house that
would have heat all winter.

My sisters were still too young to help with all the **construction**. But my mother told them, "Being little is no excuse not to pitch in." She had them squeeze juice from bags of lemons to make fresh lemonade. Then they took turns pouring and passing the cups all around.

At the end of the day there was always a lot of sweeping to do.

"I've never seen so much dust in my life," Mrs. Tran said, covering her nose.

My mother held a dustpan while I pushed the broom. My sisters giggled whenever they saw me wearing my safety mask.

Theme
Why is the family working so hard?

On Saturday nights I'd be so tired, I'd practically fall asleep right after supper.

"You're doing good work," my father would say. And he'd thank me for helping our family. He'd say, "Big dreams are built little by little, and we are making a start."

In those four months I learned a lot about putting things together. Once I even found a piece of wood that my father said I could keep. I thought that maybe I could use it to make something on my own.

One day Mr. Tran gave everyone some news. The new house would be theirs!

"Everything is beautiful," Mrs. Tran said. She stood smiling inside the framed front door. She watched her daughter paint the big front room. The kitchen had shiny linoleum floors and brand-new **appliances**. There even was a washing machine! Upstairs was a bathroom and three carpeted bedrooms. Out back there was a place for a garden.

When the Tran family moved in, they threw a potluck
supper. My father and I took care to make something extra
special that night.

"Since I've been promoted to cook, I like to whip
up a storm," he said.

We not only celebrated the Tran family's being the **owners** of their new home, but we also celebrated because we knew we were one house closer to our dream.

The hard work of many people is needed to build a home.

Former President Jimmy Carter helps build a Habitat for Humanity home.

All Over the World

Habitat for Humanity builds homes in many places besides the United States. Their work can also be seen in other countries such as Thailand, South Africa, and Guatemala. In each country, the houses are built from materials that are available nearby. That makes it easier for families to keep their homes in good shape and for the homes to look as if they fit into the neighborhood.

Features in a Textbook

Using Features in a Textbook

The following textbook features are used in this article to help you understand what you are reading.

- An **Introduction** is a brief explanation of the text.
- A **Heading** appears before a piece of writing.
- **Boldface Type** calls attention to important words.
- **Different-sized Type** shows a heading or important words.
- A **Caption** explains the photo.

Connect and Compare

1. Read the caption for the photo on page 317. Where was the photo taken? **Using Features in a Textbook**

2. Suppose that you and your family are working with Habitat for Humanity. What jobs do you think you could or would like to do? **Synthesize**

3. Think about this article and *A Castle on Viola Street*. What could you tell Andy about Habitat for Humanity that he might not have already learned? **Reading/Writing Across Texts**

Social Studies Activity

Ask your family members and friends what kinds of volunteer work they do or know about. Use your research to write a paragraph about one interesting volunteer job.

 Find out more about volunteering at **www.macmillanmh.com**

Writer's Craft

Formal Language

In a business letter, use **formal language** and be very polite. Put a colon at the end of the greeting and a comma at the end of the closing. Add periods to abbreviations in addresses, dates, and titles.

Since this is a business letter, I used formal and polite language.

I used a colon at the end of the greeting and a comma at the end of the closing.

893 Maple Ave.
Elmsville, OH 54321
May 7, 20--

Mr. John Garcia
Puppet Playhouse
1 Alton St.
Elmsville, OH 54321

Dear Mr. Garcia:

   I saw your huge ad for Puppet Playhouse in the newspaper. I would like to get information about having your puppets perform at a birthday party. Please send me helpful information and photographs.

      Sincerely yours,
      Adam L.

Your Turn

Write a business letter to a company from which you would like to get more information. Your letter could be directed to the company itself or to a person who works there. Explain why you are writing and what you need. Write in a voice that is formal and polite. Use the Writer's Checklist to check your writing.

Writer's Checklist

 Ideas and Content: Do I state what I want?

 Organization: Did I use the correct form for a business letter?

Voice: Did I use **formal language**? Was I very polite?

 Word Choice: Did I use precise nouns, adjectives, and verbs?

Sentence Fluency: Did I avoid run-on sentences?

Conventions: Did I put a colon after the greeting and a comma after the closing? Did I use abbreviations correctly and check my spelling?

Talk About It

Animals are amazing creatures. What is the most unusual thing you have ever seen an animal do?

LOG ON Find out more about unusual animals at **www.macmillanmh.com**

UNUSUAL ANIMALS

MAX
THE AMAZING HAMSTER

by Raymond So

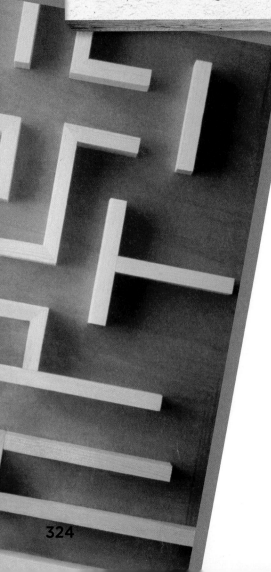

Max is my pet hamster. He's really cool and fun. One day, my brother Marco came home and picked up Max.

"The science fair is next month," he said. "I have to come up with a great project."

"That's easy," I said. "Build a volcano."

"Everyone makes volcanoes," he answered. "I want to do something really different."

I could see that our **conversation** about volcanoes was over. I stopped talking, and so did Marco. Finally, I **interrupted** the silence and said, "What about Max? Maybe you could use him for a science project."

"Max!" Marco grinned and yelled with joy. "Yes!"

Marco did some research and then turned back to me.

"I'm not **boasting**, but I think I'm really smart. I have the best plan," he said. "I'll build a maze. I'll see if Max can go through it faster in the morning or at night. Hamsters are more active at night. I think Max will be faster then. Want to help?"

I did! We built a cardboard maze, and we put a food pellet at one end and Max at the other.

At first, Max started to **sway** back and forth on his little legs, as if rocking like that would help him figure out what was happening. Then, he smelled the food. Max **scrambled** quickly toward it. When he reached it, he **seized** the pellet in his teeth.

"Max did okay, but the maze fell apart," I said. "Let's **rebuild** it. I'll get some wood."

We made the maze again. The next morning Marco started timing Max. He timed Max twice a day for two weeks—every morning and every night. It turned out that Marco was right. Max was faster at night than in the morning. That little guy is one amazing hamster!

Reread for **Comprehension**

Monitor Comprehension
Make Judgments
When you make judgments, you decide how you feel about something. You can monitor your understanding of a story or its characters when you use your own experiences to make judgments about them.

A Judgment Chart can help you judge a character's actions. Reread the selection to make judgments about the brothers' actions.

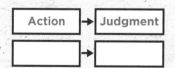

Action → Judgment

Comprehension

Genre

A **Fantasy** is a story about invented characters who could not exist in real life.

Monitor Comprehension

Make Judgments

As you read, use your Judgment Chart.

Action	→	Judgment
	→	

Read to Find Out

How would you describe Charlotte's personality?

Wilbur's Boast

from Charlotte's Web

by E. B. White

illustrated by
Garth Williams

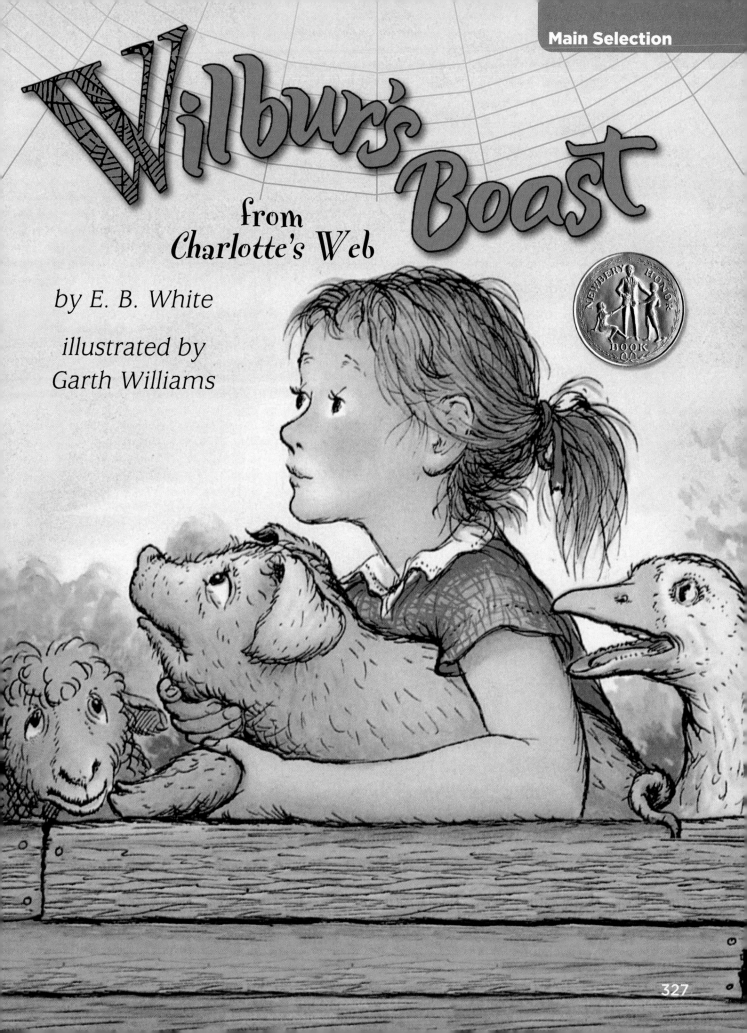

A spider's web is stronger than it looks. Although it is made of thin, delicate strands, the web is not easily broken. However, a web gets torn every day by the insects that kick around in it, and a spider must **rebuild** it when it gets full of holes. Charlotte liked to do her weaving during the late afternoon, and Fern liked to sit nearby and watch. One afternoon she heard a most interesting **conversation** and witnessed a strange event.

"You have awfully hairy legs, Charlotte," said Wilbur, as the spider busily worked at her task.

"My legs are hairy for a good reason," replied Charlotte. "Furthermore, each leg of mine has seven sections—the coxa, the trochanter, the femur, the patella, the tibia, the metatarsus, and the tarsus."

Wilbur sat bolt upright. "You're kidding," he said.

"No, I'm not, either."

"Say those names again, I didn't catch them the first time."

"Coxa, trochanter, femur, patella, tibia, metatarsus, and tarsus."

"Goodness!" said Wilbur, looking down at his own chubby legs. "I don't think *my* legs have seven sections."

Make Judgments

Does Wilbur's comment about Charlotte's legs show good manners?

"Well," said Charlotte, "you and I lead different lives. You don't have to spin a web. That takes real leg work."

"I could spin a web if I tried," said Wilbur, **boasting**. "I've just never tried."

"Let's see you do it," said Charlotte. Fern chuckled softly, and her eyes grew wide with love for the pig.

"O.K.," replied Wilbur. "You coach me and I'll spin one. It must be a lot of fun to spin a web. How do I start?"

"Take a deep breath!" said Charlotte, smiling. Wilbur breathed deeply. "Now climb to the highest place you can get to, like this." Charlotte raced up to the top of the doorway. Wilbur **scrambled** to the top of the manure pile.

"Very good!" said Charlotte. "Now make an attachment with your spinnerets, hurl yourself into space, and let out a dragline as you go down!"

Wilbur hesitated a moment, then jumped out into the air. He glanced hastily behind to see if a piece of rope was following him to check his fall, but nothing seemed to be happening in his rear, and the next thing he knew he landed with a thump. "Ooomp!" he grunted.

Charlotte laughed so hard her web began to **sway**.

"What did I do wrong?" asked the pig, when he recovered from his bump.

"Nothing," said Charlotte. "It was a nice try."

"I think I'll try again," said Wilbur, cheerfully. "I believe what I need is a little piece of string to hold me."

The pig walked out to his yard. "You there, Templeton?" he called. The rat poked his head out from under the trough.

"Got a little piece of string I could borrow?" asked Wilbur. "I need to spin a web."

"Yes, indeed," replied Templeton, who saved string. "No trouble at all. Anything to oblige." He crept down into his hole, pushed the goose egg out of the way, and returned with an old piece of dirty white string. Wilbur examined it.

"That's just the thing," he said. "Tie one end to my tail, will you, Templeton?"

Wilbur crouched low, with his thin, curly tail toward the rat. Templeton **seized** the string, passed it around the end of the pig's tail, and tied two half hitches. Charlotte watched in delight. Like Fern, she was truly fond of Wilbur, whose smelly pen and stale food attracted the flies that she needed, and she was proud to see that he was not a quitter and was willing to try again to spin a web.

While the rat and the spider and the little girl watched, Wilbur climbed again to the top of the manure pile, full of energy and hope.

"Everybody watch!" he cried. And summoning all his strength, he threw himself into the air, headfirst. The string trailed behind him. But as he had neglected to fasten the other end to anything, it didn't really do any good, and Wilbur landed with a thud, crushed and hurt. Tears came to his eyes. Templeton grinned. Charlotte just sat quietly. After a bit she spoke.

"You can't spin a web, Wilbur, and I advise you to put the idea out of your mind. You lack two things needed for spinning a web."

"What are they?" asked Wilbur, sadly.

"You lack a set of spinnerets, and you lack know-how. But cheer up, you don't need a web. Zuckerman supplies you with three big meals a day. Why should you worry about trapping food?"

Wilbur sighed. "You're ever so much cleverer and brighter than I am, Charlotte. I guess I was just trying to show off. Serves me right."

Templeton untied his string and took it back to his home. Charlotte returned to her weaving.

"You needn't feel too badly, Wilbur," she said. "Not many creatures can spin webs. Even men aren't as good at it as spiders, although they *think* they're pretty good, and they'll *try* anything. Did you ever hear of the Queensborough Bridge?"

Wilbur shook his head. "Is it a web?"

"Sort of," replied Charlotte. "But do you know how long it took men to build it? Eight whole years. My goodness, I would have starved to death waiting that long. I can make a web in a single evening."

"What do people catch in the Queensborough Bridge—bugs?" asked Wilbur.

"No," said Charlotte. "They don't catch anything. They just keep trotting back and forth across the bridge thinking there is something better on the other side. If they'd hang head-down at the top of the thing and wait quietly, maybe something good would come along. But no—with men it's rush, rush, rush, every minute. I'm glad I'm a sedentary spider."

"What does sedentary mean?" asked Wilbur.

"Means I sit still a good part of the time and don't go wandering all over creation. I know a good thing when I see it, and my web is a good thing. I stay put and wait for what comes. Gives me a chance to think."

"Well, I'm sort of sedentary myself, I guess," said the pig. "I have to hang around here whether I want to or not. You know where I'd really like to be this evening?"

"Where?"

"In a forest looking for beechnuts and truffles and delectable roots, pushing leaves aside with my wonderful strong nose, searching and sniffing along the ground, smelling, smelling, smelling ... "

"You smell just the way you are," remarked a lamb who had just walked in. "I can smell you from here. You're the smelliest creature in the place."

Wilbur hung his head. His eyes grew wet with tears. Charlotte noticed his embarrassment and she spoke sharply to the lamb.

"Let Wilbur alone!" she said. "He has a perfect right to smell, considering his surroundings. You're no bundle of sweet peas yourself. Furthermore, you are interrupting a very pleasant conversation. What were we talking about, Wilbur, when we were so rudely **interrupted**?"

"Oh, I don't remember," said Wilbur. "It doesn't make any difference. Let's not talk any more for a while, Charlotte. I'm getting sleepy. You go ahead and finish fixing your web and I'll just lie here and watch you. It's a lovely evening." Wilbur stretched out on his side.

Twilight settled over Zuckerman's barn, and a feeling of peace.

Make Judgments
Do you think Charlotte really wants to make Wilbur feel better? Why or why not?

Spin a Web with
E. B. and Garth

AUTHOR

E. B. White had a farm very much like the one in this story. One day when E. B. was going to feed his pig, he began to feel sad. He did not want his pig to be killed. E. B. thought about how to save him. While he was thinking, he saw a big spider spinning a web. Soon E. B. was spinning the novel *Charlotte's Web*.

Other books by E. B. White:
Stuart Little and *The Trumpet of the Swan*

ILLUSTRATOR

Garth Williams has said that *Charlotte's Web* was one of his favorite books to illustrate. Garth did the pictures while he was living on a farm. He based his illustrations on what he saw around him. He drew the animals over and over again until they seemed to look like people.

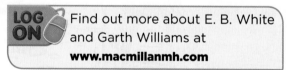

LOG ON Find out more about E. B. White and Garth Williams at **www.macmillanmh.com**

Author's Purpose

What was E. B. White's main purpose for writing?
Explain how you can tell.

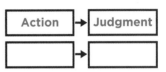

Comprehension Check

Summarize

Use your Judgment Chart to help you summarize *Wilbur's Boast*. Tell about an important event in the selection by showing evidence from the story, making inferences based on that information, and describing how the event ends.

Action		Judgment
	→	
	→	

Think and Compare

1. Think about Wilbur's **boasting** and his attempts to spin a web. Were these attempts smart? Include story details in your answer. **Monitor Comprehension: Make Judgments**

2. Reread page 330. Why do you think Charlotte tells Wilbur how to spin a web? Use story details in your answer. **Analyze**

3. If you were to meet Charlotte, what questions would you ask her about the meaning of friendship? **Apply**

4. Why do you think that Charlotte says humans rush around too much? Explain your answer. **Evaluate**

5. Read "Max, the Amazing Hamster" on pages 324-325. Compare the way animals are shown in this story and in *Wilbur's Boast*. Which is realistic and which is fantasy? Use details from both selections to explain your answer. **Reading/Writing Across Texts**

Do Animals Have Personalities?

by Patricia West

Everyone has a **personality**, or a unique way of acting and thinking. One person might love to run and jump. Another may prefer to sit and think. Your next-door neighbor could be very shy, but your cousin may be friendly to everyone. Each of these people has a different personality.

Animals also have personalities. Scientists study their **behavior**, or the way they act, in order to learn more about them. Here are three **individual** animals that have special personalities.

What a Bell Can Tell

A cat named Phoenix doesn't need anyone to open doors for him. When he wants to go out, he just pushes a special doorbell.

The doorbell's inventor thought that many people would rush to buy cat doorbells, but few have been sold. That may be because not many cats have the same independent personality as Phoenix.

SKILL

Following Directions

Here's an experiment to find out something interesting about a cat. It will tell you whether a cat is "right-pawed" or "left-pawed."

Is Your Cat Right-Pawed or Left-Pawed?

What to Do

1. Use the spoon to put a little cat food in the bottle.

2. Put the bottle on its side near the cat.

3. When the cat uses its paw to get the food, write down whether the cat uses its right or left paw.

4. Repeat Steps 1-3 several times.

5. Count the number of times the cat uses its right paw and the number of times it uses its left paw.

6. Decide whether your cat is right-pawed, left-pawed, or both.

What You Need

- a hungry cat
- a small, empty plastic bottle with a narrow opening just big enough for the cat's paw
- a little food that the cat likes
- a spoon

Pumpkin Play

Scientists at Seattle's Woodland Park Zoo gave carved pumpkins to their gorillas. They observed how their gorillas played with the pumpkins before eating them.

A gorilla called Zuri grabbed as many pumpkins as he could. Another gorilla, Jumoke, spent a lot of time picking out the biggest pumpkin. Alafia looked for a pumpkin she could fit over her head. Congo chose a pumpkin with a face he liked best. Each gorilla showed his or her personality while making choices.

Brilliant Birdbrain

Most parrots can only repeat words their owners say, but one parrot, named Alex, is a talker *and* a good listener! When his owner holds up a tray with different objects, Alex can pick out the yellow object, the biggest object, or even "the one under the square."

Alex also has a good memory. If his owner asks, "Alex, what color is corn?" Alex answers, "Yellow." He can do this even if there is no corn in sight to give him a hint.

Connect and Compare

1. Look at the directions for the experiment on page 341. Explain the directions in Step 4. **Following Directions**

2. Do you know any pets that seem to have interesting personalities? Explain. **Analyze**

3. Which animals in "Wilbur's Boast" remind you of animals in this selection? Use details from both selections in your answer. **Reading/Writing Across Texts**

Science Activity

Choose an animal you know. Observe the animal to learn more about it. Then write a paragraph that tells three new things you learned in your research.

 Find out more about unusual animals at
www.macmillanmh.com

Write a News Story

My first sentence tells who, what, when, where, and why.

My news story includes transition words such as "because."

Elephant Friends

by Junko N.

Almost 22 years ago, two elephants named Jenny and Shirley met at a circus where they both performed. Then they were separated. Recently Jenny and Shirley met again because they were reunited at the Elephant Sanctuary in Tennessee.

When Jenny and Shirley saw each other, they started roaring and tried to climb in each other's pens. The people at the sanctuary never saw elephants get so excited. As a result, they put them in the same pen. Now, Jenny and Shirley seem happier than ever because of the sanctuary staff's efforts.

Your Turn

Research and write a news story about an animal. You can use magazines and newspapers, or do research on the Internet with an adult's help. As you research and write, think about the five *W*s. In your first sentence, explain *Who*, *What*, *When*, *Where*, and *Why*. In the story, use transition words and at least one adjective that compares, such as *happier*. Use the Writer's Checklist to check your writing.

Writer's Checklist

✓ **Ideas and Content:** Is my news story about a real event?

✓ **Organization:** Does my news story have a topic sentence and supporting details?

✓ **Voice:** Does my news story tell the facts without showing my feelings?

☐ **Word Choice:** Did I use **transition words**?

✓ **Sentence Fluency:** Did I vary the lengths of my sentences?

✓ **Conventions:** Did I use the correct forms of adjectives that compare? Did I check my spelling?

Talk About It

What does it mean to be a good citizen?

 Find out more about citizenship at **www.macmillanmh.com**

GOOD CITIZENS

We the People

Vocabulary

historical

dispute

automatically

requirements

Pledging Allegiance

October 12, 1892. Do you know the **historical** importance of that date? It was Columbus Day, and on that day 12 million kids in the United States recited the Pledge of Allegiance for the first time.

The original pledge was published in the September 8, 1892, issue of a Boston magazine called *The Youth's Companion.* For years there was a **dispute** over who wrote the pledge. Was it James B. Upham or Francis Bellamy? Both were members of the magazine's staff. Bellamy's son gathered documents and statements to prove that his father was the pledge's author. It paid off. In 1939 the United States Flag Association decided that Bellamy deserved the credit.

THE ORIGINAL VERSION OF THE PLEDGE:

"I pledge allegiance to my Flag and the Republic for which it stands—one nation indivisible—with liberty and justice for all."

CHANGES TO THE PLEDGE:

★ In 1923, at the first National Flag Conference, the words "my Flag" were changed to "the Flag of the United States of America."

★ Congress officially recognized the Pledge of Allegiance in 1942.

★ On Flag Day in 1954, President Dwight D. Eisenhower suggested adding the words "under God." Congress agreed, and the phrase was added.

Becoming a Citizen

Citizens of the United States have certain rights and responsibilities. When people move to the United States from other countries, they do not **automatically** become American citizens. They must fill out an application with the Immigration and Naturalization Service. They must meet certain **requirements**, such as being able to read, write, and speak ordinary English. They must also pass a test on the history and government of the United States. After they become citizens, they have the right to vote and hold public office.

LOG ON Find out more about becoming a U.S. citizen at **www.macmillanmh.com**

Top 5 States with the Most Hispanics

There are more than 30 million Hispanic people living in the United States. Every year Hispanic Heritage Month begins on September 15, which marks the date when five Latin American countries gained independence: Costa Rica, El Salvador, Guatemala, Honduras, and Nicaragua.

Eight out of ten Hispanics in the U.S. live in these five states.

1. California	**11,980,884**
2. Texas	**7,614,414**
3. Florida	**3,108,578**
4. New York	**3,034,124**
5. Illinois	**1,694,185**

Source: U.S. Census Bureau, 2003

Comprehension

Genre
A **Nonfiction Article** gives information about real people, places, or things.

Analyze Text Structure
Problem and Solution
A problem is something that needs to be worked out. A solution is something that fixes a problem.

An American Hero Flies Again

How did one astronaut help science twice?

The idea of a person flying into space was a dream until the 1950s. That's when United States and Soviet Union scientists began a space race to make the dream a reality. The Soviet Union pulled ahead, launching two satellites, *Sputnik 1* and *Sputnik 2*, into space in 1957. The U.S. needed a plan to catch up. The National Aeronautics and Space Administration (NASA) was formed to put an astronaut into space. John Glenn would be that astronaut.

John Glenn in 1998

The mission to get a manned spacecraft into orbit was called Project Mercury. Scientists at NASA raced to get a spacecraft ready for launch, but the Soviet Union beat the U.S. again when Yuri Gagarin, a Soviet cosmonaut, orbited Earth in 1961. Ten months later, Glenn climbed aboard the 10-foot-long *Friendship 7* and became the first American to circle Earth in a spacecraft. The U.S. had finally caught up with the Soviet Union in the space race.

Glenn's flight lasted only 4 hours, 55 minutes, 23 seconds from liftoff to touchdown back to Earth. During that time, Glenn orbited Earth three times. It was a historic mission. However, this was not the end of the space race. The next step was getting the first person on the moon. Glenn worked on the cockpit layout and control functions on the Apollo Project. His efforts helped get U.S. astronaut Neil Armstrong to the moon on July 20, 1969.

Glenn was already a hero when he served his country as a fighter pilot in World War II, but at NASA, he was a hero to science. After leaving NASA, Glenn served his country as a U.S. senator. Then in 1998, at age 77, Senator Glenn would get his chance to help science again.

In 1962 an Atlas rocket carried John Glenn and *Friendship 7* into space.

Discovery Mission

NASA scientists needed to find out the best way to study the effects of aging on the body. They needed a qualified older astronaut who was healthy enough to make the trip. That person would also launch a spacecraft to study the heat and winds surrounding the sun. Again, Glenn was chosen.

On board the STS-95 *Discovery*, Glenn wore monitors on his chest and head to measure changes in his heartbeat and brain waves. As people grow older, they experience physical problems, such as loss of balance and muscle tone. The conditions in space have similar effects on astronauts. Because John Glenn wore monitors, scientists today can study the **historical** data of his trip. This data helps scientists understand aging better.

Ready, Set, Blast Off!

Glenn wasn't **automatically** accepted for the 1998 mission. First, he had to pass physical tests to make sure he was healthy enough. Then he had months of preparation. One of the **requirements** was the ability to save himself in case of an emergency. Glenn admits that he was creakier than the rest of the crew. "I don't bend in the same directions they bend," he said.

Glenn (third from left) and his *Discovery* crewmates

Studying an Aging Astronaut

	1962	1998
JOHN GLENN		
Height:	5 feet 10 inches	5 feet 10 inches
Hair color:	Red	White
Age:	40	77
THE SPACECRAFT		
Name:	*Friendship 7*	*Discovery*
Crew size:	1	7
Windows:	1	10
Computers:	0	5
Weight:	4,256 pounds	153,819 pounds
THE MISSION		
Name:	Mercury 6	STS-95
Launch date:	February 20, 1962	October 29, 1998
Duration:	4 hr. 55 min. 23 sec.	8 days 21 hr. 44 min.
Distance flown:	75,679 miles	3,680,000 miles

As Glenn got ready to board *Discovery*, thousands of excited fans cheered him on. Among them were Daniel and Zach Glenn, the astronaut's grandsons. "It's a little scary," admitted Dan, 16, "but pretty neat that he went up so long ago and is going up again." Zach, 13, said, "He is a great guy and a really nice grandpa. He's an American hero." There's no **dispute** about that.

Think and Compare

1. What problem did the U.S. face with the space program in 1961?

2. In what three ways did John Glenn serve his country?

3. Why do you think John Glenn is described as a hero?

4. How does each of these selections relate to the theme of "good citizens"?

Test Strategy

Think and Search

The answer is in more than one place. Keep reading to find the answer.

Who Is Uncle Sam?

★ ★ ★ ★ ★ ★ ★ ★ ★ ★ ★

Uncle Sam was already a well-known symbol of the United States when he appeared on this World War I recruiting poster.

I WANT YOU FOR U.S. ARMY

NEAREST RECRUITING STATION

He has a long white beard. He wears a tall hat and a red, white, and blue suit. He is Uncle Sam, and he is a symbol of the U. S. government. Is Uncle Sam a made-up cartoon character? Or is he based on a real person?

One idea is that Uncle Sam was named after a man named Samuel Wilson. During the War of 1812, Wilson sold meat to the U.S. Army. The meat was packed in barrels stamped with the letters *U.S.* Some people joked that *U.S.* stood for "Uncle Sam" Wilson.

In 1838 Thomas Nast created a picture of Uncle Sam. Nast drew political cartoons. In these cartoons, Uncle Sam has a beard. Samuel Wilson, who didn't have a beard, was probably not Nast's model.

By 1916 the United States was at war again. James Flagg painted a poster to get people to join the Army. On it, a determined-looking Uncle Sam points and says, "I WANT YOU." To this day, Uncle Sam is a symbol for American strength and determination.

Go On ▶

Directions: Answer the questions.

1. Why is Uncle Sam a symbol of the U.S. government?

A Government leaders look like him.

B He was created long ago.

C He looks determined, and he wears red, white, and blue.

D His picture appears on the U.S. flag.

2. James Flagg created his Uncle Sam poster for

A meat-buyers for the U.S. Army.

B people who did not live in the United States.

C people who could help fight the war.

D newspaper reporters.

Tip
Keep reading.
The answer is
in more than
one place.

3. Which statement BEST summarizes the main idea of the article?

A Uncle Sam provided meat for the U.S. Army.

B Uncle Sam was definitely a real person.

C Uncle Sam is a famous United States symbol.

D Government property is stamped with Uncle Sam's picture.

4. Why is it hard to prove that Uncle Sam was named after Samuel Wilson?

5. How do you think Thomas Nast chose Uncle Sam's costume? Explain why he chose the colors and design. Use details to support your response.

Write to a Prompt

Imagine that you go to the playground and find someone making fun of a new kid. The new kid, Juan, speaks only Spanish. He looks sad and scared. Write a story of at least three paragraphs about what you do and say that shows good citizenship. Tell what happens next.

I put events in order to organize my writing.

Juan, Grant, and Me

Juan just came to our school. I can talk to him in Spanish, but he doesn't speak English very well yet. When I got to the playground, Grant was saying mean things to Juan. Grant seemed mad. Juan looked scared.

I didn't like what Grant was doing. I said, "Grant! Knock it off! Why are you being so mean?" Grant stopped, but he still looked mean. "Juan is a really good guy, and he's great at soccer," I said. Grant stopped frowning. He knew that we needed another player for our team.

Juan smiled at me. "Gracias," he said.

"De nada," I said. Then I kicked the ball toward him. Juan got the ball and kicked it to Grant. We all had a great time after that.

Writing Prompt

Being a good citizen can mean a lot of different things. Think about what it means to you. Then write a story that tells how someone learned what being a good citizen means. Your story should have at least three paragraphs.

Writer's Checklist

☑ Ask yourself, who will read my story?

☑ Think about your purpose for writing.

☑ Plan your writing before beginning.

☑ Use details to support your story.

☑ Be sure your story has a beginning, a middle, and an ending.

WORKING TOGETHER

Talk About It

How can animals help people at work and in their daily lives?

LOG ON Find out more about working together at **www.macmillanmh.com**

Dogs for the Deaf

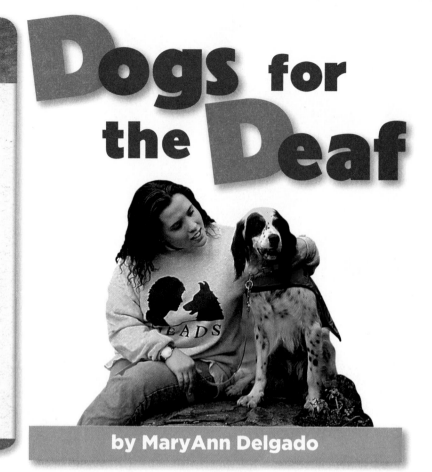

by MaryAnn Delgado

When a fire alarm goes off, you know it! The sound alerts you to danger. What if you were deaf? How would you know if an alarm went off, or if someone knocked on your door? If you took a walk and **strolled** across a busy street, you wouldn't hear if a car beeped at you. A signal dog could help you with all of these things!

Helping Ears

Signal dogs are also called hearing ear dogs. They help people who are deaf by acting as their owners' "ears."

They know what to do when they hear certain sounds. These dogs can learn up to eight sounds, including sounds from sirens, doorbells, and crying babies.

How They Help

Babies cry at night for many reasons. They might be hungry, lonely, or wet. When they cry, the sound is **pitiful**! Even extremely **sleepy** parents will wake up quickly to help. But what if a mom and dad can't hear? That's when a signal dog can help.

The dog can quickly wake his owner. He might nudge him with his nose, or pull at his night clothes. When his owner wakes up, the dog runs to the baby. The dog may **crouch** down near the crib. If his owner doesn't follow, the dog does it again.

The dog will run back and forth until his owner takes action. A signal dog does different things for each sound it knows.

Kinds of Dogs

There is no **official** kind of hearing ear dog. Many sizes and breeds can be trained. Some dogs are short and fluffy. Others are tall, thin, and **sleek**. They may not all move with beauty and **grace**, but all signal dogs are smart!

Large dogs are better in public places because they won't get stepped on. Small dogs, however, can jump in your lap. Why is that important? Because signal dogs are more than just "ears." They are also friends.

Reread for **Comprehension**

Monitor Comprehension
Author's Purpose

As you read, remember to monitor your comprehension. To help check your understanding of an article, think about the author's purpose.

An Author's Purpose Chart helps you identify clues to the author's purpose and helps you understand what you read. Reread the selection to learn the author's purpose.

Clues

↓

Author's Purpose

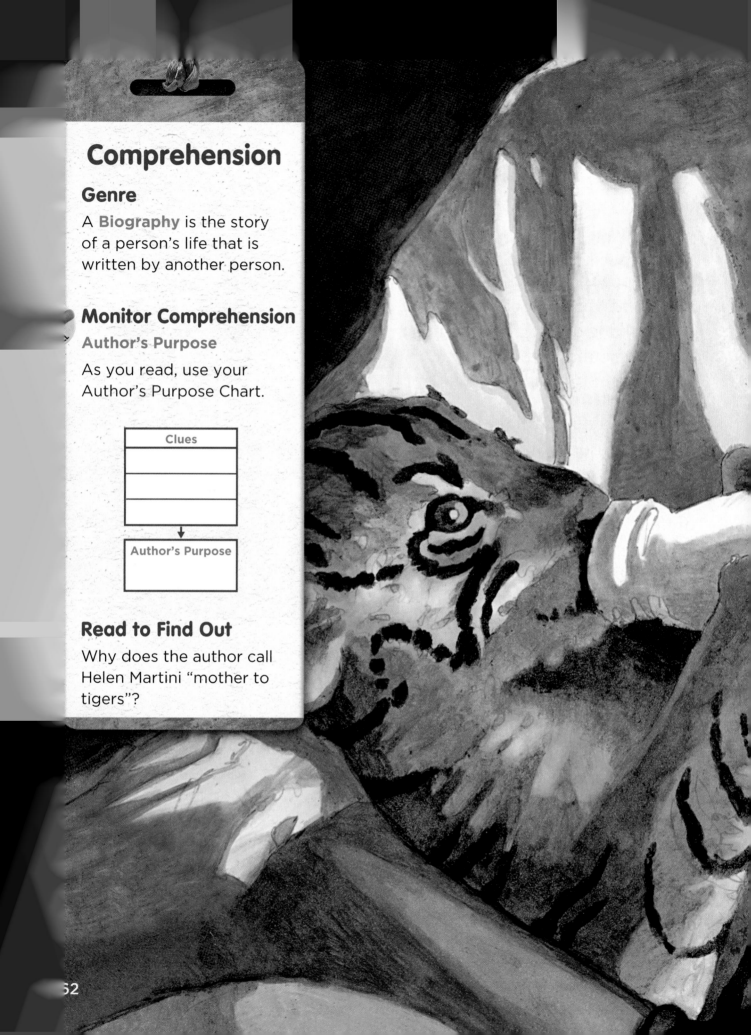

Comprehension

Genre
A **Biography** is the story of a person's life that is written by another person.

Monitor Comprehension
Author's Purpose

As you read, use your Author's Purpose Chart.

Clues

↓

Author's Purpose

Read to Find Out
Why does the author call Helen Martini "mother to tigers"?

Award Winning Selection

Mother to Tigers

by George Ella Lyon
illustrations by Peter Catalanotto

Suppose you were a lion cub—abandoned.
Suppose you lay hungry and cold
in the straw at the back of the den,

and a man came in the cage
and lifted you into a case

and put you in a car
to go home with him.

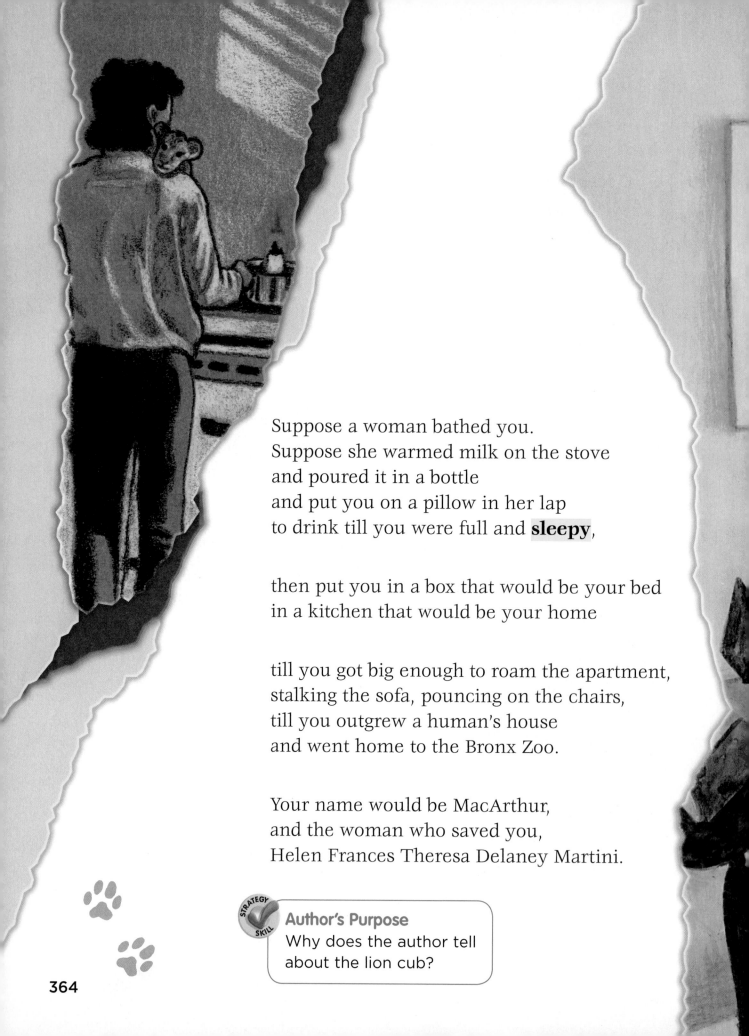

Suppose a woman bathed you.
Suppose she warmed milk on the stove
and poured it in a bottle
and put you on a pillow in her lap
to drink till you were full and **sleepy**,

then put you in a box that would be your bed
in a kitchen that would be your home

till you got big enough to roam the apartment,
stalking the sofa, pouncing on the chairs,
till you outgrew a human's house
and went home to the Bronx Zoo.

Your name would be MacArthur,
and the woman who saved you,
Helen Frances Theresa Delaney Martini.

Author's Purpose
Why does the author tell
about the lion cub?

364

Helen never planned to raise cubs.
She and her husband, Fred, wanted children.
But their first baby died,
and doctors said she couldn't have more.

To ease their hurt hearts,
they collected pets: a parrot, a dog,
a starling, and twelve canaries.

Before long, their little apartment
was full of song and feathers.

On weekends, when Fred was free
from his job as a jeweler,
they **strolled** through the Bronx Zoo,
just down the street from their house.

Fred loved those times—
watching polar bears dive
and elephants amble,
studying the **grace** of giraffes.
Finally Helen said,
"Why don't you follow your heart
and work at the Zoo?"
So he did.

Each night he brought home questions
about animals he cared for,
and together he and Helen would read and learn.

When he brought MacArthur home
to the apartment on Old Kingsbridge Road,
the cub was a **pitiful** sight.
"Just do for him what you would do
for a human baby," Fred told Helen.
And she did.

After MacArthur
came Dacca, Rajpur, and Raniganj,
a litter of Bengal tigers.

Rajpur was so cold and thin,
Helen thought he might die,
but she put him on a heating pad
and sat by him for hours
moistening his mouth with milk.
At last he gave a weak cry.
Helen almost cried too.

Feeding three was a challenge!
Helen wished she were an octopus.
But before long those scrawny babies
were **sleek**, fat cubs, ready to romp.

Once, washing clothes in the bath,
Helen heard Raniganj crying.
His head was caught behind a pipe.
While she ran to the rescue,

Rajpur and Dacca discovered the tub.
Crouch ... leap ... *splash!*
Tigers love water.

When the striped trio
had to go back to the Zoo,
they still needed their bottles,
so Helen brought a hot plate
and set up a little kitchen
in the sleeping room
at the back of their cage.

The first night, she and Fred
ate their dinner there too.
Helen didn't want to leave
till her cubs were fast asleep.

371

Come daybreak, she was back
and she was thinking:
These tigers will grow up,
but there will always be zoo babies
who need special care.
She couldn't take all of them home,
but she could bring home to them.
She could start a nursery at the Zoo!

"Just give me a room," she said
to Mr. Crandall, the man in charge.
"I'll do all the work."
And she did.

She cleaned and plastered a storeroom,
which she painted pink and blue.

Then she begged, borrowed, and bought
everything she needed.

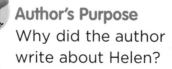

STRATEGY SKILL

Author's Purpose
Why did the author
write about Helen?

Starting out, she didn't get paid,
but that wasn't what mattered.
She was following her heart,
and her nursery filled up quickly.

Soon it was **official**:
She was the first woman keeper
in the history of the Bronx Zoo.

Before Helen arrived,
no tiger born at the Zoo had ever survived.
She raised twenty-seven,

along with yapoks and marmosets,
gorillas and chimpanzees,
deer and ring-tailed lemurs.

She still took cubs home, too:
lions, tigers,
jaguars, and a black leopard.

Helen's cubs had cubs
that were sent to zoos
all around the world.
The idea of the nursery spread too.

So, wherever you live,
when you go to the zoo,
look hard at the mighty cats.

Their grandparents
may have opened their eyes
on Old Kingsbridge Road,

may have learned to walk
in that apartment kitchen,

saved
by Helen Frances Theresa Delaney Martini,
mother to tigers.

Roar with George and Peter

AUTHOR

George Ella Lyon first learned about Helen Martini when she was 10 years old. She read Helen's book and began to think about becoming a zookeeper. The next year, George Ella was lucky enough to take a trip to New York and visit the Bronx Zoo. She did not get to meet Helen, but she did see some of her cats.

ILLUSTRATOR

Peter Catalanotto had a lot of practice to illustrate this book. When he was a boy, he spent most of his time down in his basement drawing animals. Today Peter illustrates books by other people and has written some of his own books.

Other books by George Ella Lyon: *Come a Tide* and *Mama Is a Miner*

 Find out more about George Ella Lyon and Peter Catalanotto at **www.macmillanmh.com**

Author's Purpose

Which parts of this biography by George Ella Lyon did you find most informative? Did she also write to entertain readers? Explain.

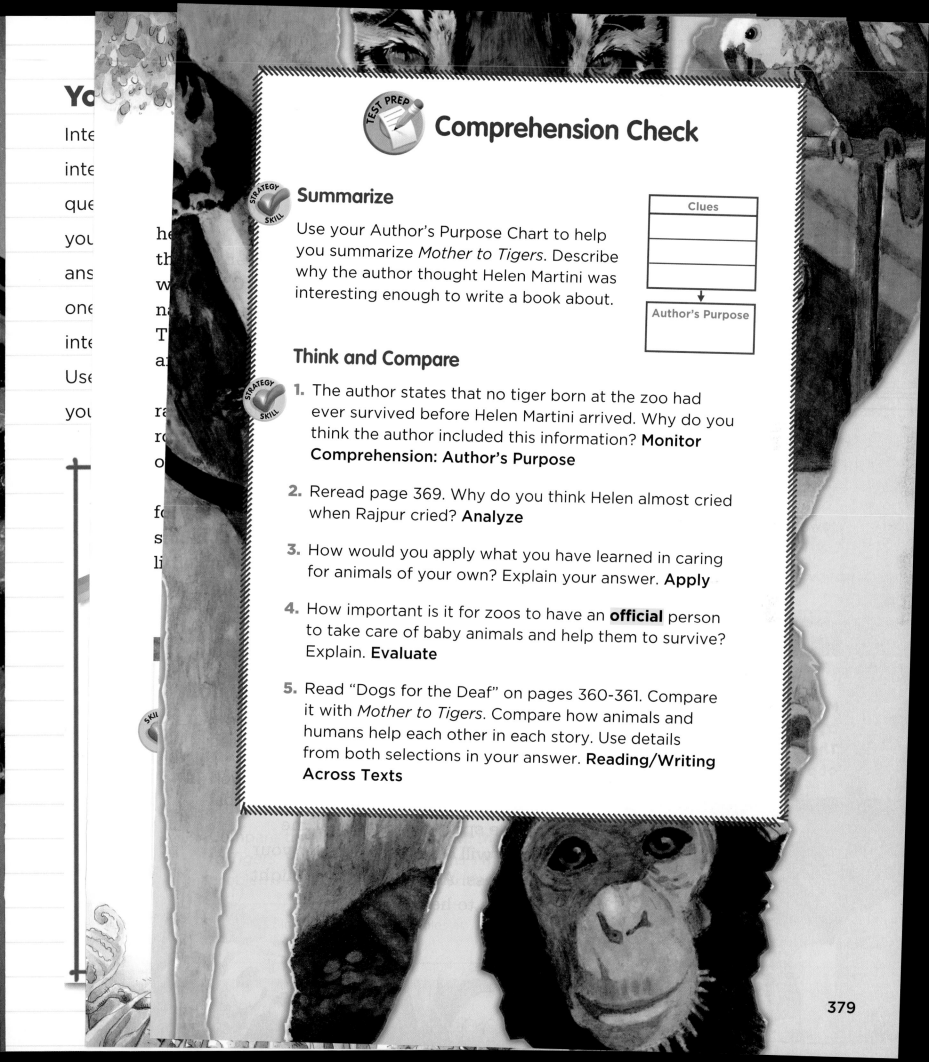

Comprehension Check

TEST PREP

Summarize

STRATEGY SKILL

Use your Author's Purpose Chart to help you summarize *Mother to Tigers*. Describe why the author thought Helen Martini was interesting enough to write a book about.

Clues

↓

Author's Purpose

Think and Compare

STRATEGY SKILL

1. The author states that no tiger born at the zoo had ever survived before Helen Martini arrived. Why do you think the author included this information? **Monitor Comprehension: Author's Purpose**

2. Reread page 369. Why do you think Helen almost cried when Rajpur cried? **Analyze**

3. How would you apply what you have learned in caring for animals of your own? Explain your answer. **Apply**

4. How important is it for zoos to have an **official** person to take care of baby animals and help them to survive? Explain. **Evaluate**

5. Read "Dogs for the Deaf" on pages 360-361. Compare it with *Mother to Tigers*. Compare how animals and humans help each other in each story. Use details from both selections in your answer. **Reading/Writing Across Texts**

Vocabulary

disappear   supply

protect   capture

harming   enclosure

involved

Dictionary

Multiple-Meaning Words have more than one meaning. Use a dictionary to find the correct meaning of the word *enclosure* in the last paragraph.

Save Our Butterflies

by Sean Bryant

Scientists who study insects believe that something is happening to our butterflies. They say that 30 years ago, there were about twice as many butterflies as there are today. Where have all the butterflies gone?

The Problem

No one hurts butterflies on purpose. Still, scientists think that people have caused the butterfly problem. Butterflies find their food in wildflowers. When people clear the land for roads and buildings, these flowers **disappear**.

Some insects eat and destroy farmers' crops. Farmers use pesticides, or poisons, to get rid of harmful insects. Pesticides **protect** crops, but sometimes end up **harming** helpful insects such as caterpillars. Caterpillars turn into butterflies. This is another reason there are fewer butterflies now than in the past.

How to Help

Luckily, there are ways that kids and grownups can help. Do you want to get **involved** and help save our butterflies?

One thing you can do is plant a garden. Make sure the garden has a good **supply** of the food butterflies eat when they are caterpillars. Different kinds of caterpillars eat different plants. Monarch butterfly caterpillars eat milkweed. Black swallowtail caterpillars eat parsley, dill, or carrot leaves. Find out what kind of butterflies live in your area and plant the kinds of food they eat as caterpillars. Make sure that pesticides are not used nearby.

One More Thing

Some kids like to **capture** butterflies with nets. Then they put them in a jar or other **enclosure**. Unfortunately, it is easy to hurt a butterfly when you catch it. Its wings are torn easily. Instead, enjoy these beautiful insects from a distance.

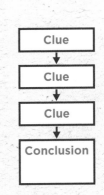

Reread for **Comprehension**

Monitor Comprehension
Draw Conclusions

Authors don't always tell readers everything. Good readers use clues from an article and what they already know to better understand what they read.

A Conclusion Map helps you find clues to information that is not stated and helps you monitor your understanding. Reread the selection to draw a conclusion about why planting a garden can save butterflies.

Clue
↓
Clue
↓
Clue
↓
Conclusion

Comprehension

Genre

A **Nonfiction Article** gives information about real people, places or things.

Monitor Comprehension

Draw Conclusions

As you read, use your Conclusion Map.

Clue
↓
Clue
↓
Clue
↓
Conclusion

Read to Find Out

How has growing butterflies helped the community?

HOME-GROWN BUTTERFLIES

by Deborah Churchman

People in Barra del Colorado, a village in Costa Rica, had a big problem. For many years, the villagers had caught fish for a living. But then, because of pollution and overfishing, the fish began to **disappear**. Soon it became hard for the people to catch enough fish to feed to their families and sell for money. What could they do?

The village is on the edge of a beautiful rainforest. One thing the villagers could have done was chop down the trees. Then they could have sold the wood and farmed the land. They would have made money but destroyed the rainforest.

A scientist named Brent Davies had another idea about how the villagers could use the rainforest. And it would keep the forest alive. The villagers could raise and sell *butterflies*.

◀ School children in Barra del Colorado are now experts at spotting caterpillars.

▼ Brent Davies and local students admire a sign that notes—in Spanish and English—they are raising insects.

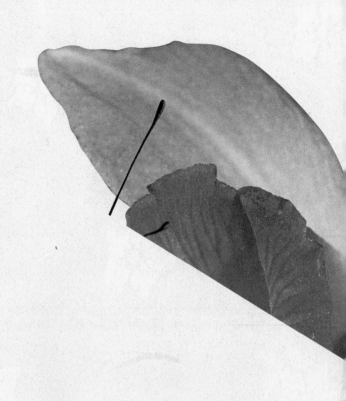

Many colorful butterflies flit around in the forest near Barra del Colorado. It would be easy to **capture** a few and use them to raise many more.

Brent knew that butterfly zoos around the world would pay for farm-raised butterflies. If the villagers could make money by selling them, they'd have a good reason to **protect** the insects' rainforest home. After all, without the forest, there would be no wild butterflies to capture. And without a steady **supply** of wild butterflies, the farm would fail.

Brent wanted to show villagers how to raise butterflies to sell. And she knew just who could help: the school kids! If adults saw kids making money with butterflies, they might want to start their own farm—and protect the forest.

Draw Conclusions
What kind of person is Brent Davies? How do you know?

SCHOOLYARD FARM

Butterflies drink nectar from certain flowers, and they lay their eggs on other plants. When the eggs hatch, caterpillars come out and eat those plants. They eat and grow, and grow and eat. When they've grown enough, the caterpillars turn into pupae (PEW-pee). And those are what butterfly zoos buy.

Brent knew that villagers could find some pupae in the rainforest to sell. But if the people could get butterflies to lay eggs in one place, they could *raise* caterpillars—and get many more pupae.

They could even let some of the extra butterflies they raised go free in the rainforest. That would make sure the forest would always have plenty.

So, how to get started? To attract butterflies, Brent figured the villagers needed a garden full of nectar plants. They also needed an **enclosure** full of plants for caterpillars to eat. She talked to people at the school. Together they decided on a good spot in the schoolyard.

Inside an enclosed area, visitors can see plants grown for hungry caterpillars.

CLEARING AND PLANTING

First they had to clear a lot of trash out of the schoolyard. The kids pitched in and stuffed more than 100 sacks with trash. Soon people were stopping by to admire their work.

Then everyone helped dig up the soil so that plants could grow. That turned up lots of worms—which attracted lots of chickens. So the kids went on "chicken patrol," chasing the birds away. Their butterfly garden needed those worms!

Next, they planted flowers to attract the butterflies. Beside the flower garden, they built the enclosure for raising caterpillars. Then they put the right kinds of plants inside it.

RAISING BUTTERFLIES

Butterflies from the forest flew to the garden to feed on the flowers. Brent taught the children how to capture the butterflies and take them into the enclosure. There, the butterflies laid tiny eggs on the special plants.

Brent also taught the children how to find caterpillars and eggs. (Some eggs are no bigger than the period at the end of this sentence.)

The kids learned to lift up leaves and look around the plants. They put the eggs and caterpillars they found into special feeding boxes. That way they could make sure the insects got plenty to eat.

Draw Conclusions
Why is it important for the kids to find as many eggs and caterpillars as possible?

◀ **Two handfuls of owl butterfly caterpillars are moved to a feeding box.**

After caterpillars turn into pupae, they are ▶ packed into boxes and shipped to zoos.

Blue morpho butterflies are bestsellers. Their wings have "eyespots" on the underside, but the topside is bright blue.

In the boxes, the caterpillars fattened up on leaves. Then they turned into pupae. The kids picked the pupae just as if they were picking a crop. They let some of the pupae turn into butterflies, and they put those back into the rainforest. But they sold the other pupae.

Today, the farm sells about 250 pupae every month. The money that's earned goes to the school for materials and equipment. The first thing the kids bought was a ceiling fan so their schoolroom wouldn't be so hot!

The best news is that some adults in the village have started doing what the kids have done—making farms for butterflies. They've learned from the kids how to use the forest without **harming** it.

The bottom blue morpho butterfly has just crawled out of its pupae case. The top one has been out for half an hour.

395

Kids in San Pasqual, California, gather eggs from plants outside their butterfly farm's enclosure.

MEANWHILE, BACK HOME

People at the San Diego Wild Animal Park helped start the butterfly farm in Costa Rica. Then they had another wild idea. Why not start this kind of farm at home in California?

They asked students at San Pasqual Union Elementary School if they wanted to get **involved**. People at the school agreed to do the same thing as the villagers in Costa Rica.

Kids and adults set up a butterfly garden and an enclosed area. Some of the money they earn pays for special things for their school, such as science equipment.

Students from California have started writing to the students in Costa Rica about their butterfly businesses. Both groups of kids feel great about what they're doing for nature!

Charlie Hanscom is just one of the kids raising money for San Pasqual Union Elementary School by helping with the butterfly farm.

FLY AWAY WITH DEBORAH

REPORTER DEBORAH CHURCHMAN grew up next to a creek in the suburbs near Washington, D.C. Now she grows butterfly bushes and other wildlife-attracting plants in her yard for the enjoyment of her four kids and granddaughter. Deborah is a senior editor at *Ranger Rick,* where she writes articles about nature every day.

 Find out more about Deborah Churchman at **www.macmillanmh.com**

Author's Purpose

What was Deborah Churchman's purpose for writing *Home-Grown Butterflies*? Did she want to entertain, inform, or persuade readers with this nonfiction article? How do you know?

Comprehension Check

Summarize

Use the Conclusion Map to help you summarize "Home-Grown Butterflies." Explain whether or not the children were able to help their community by growing butterflies.

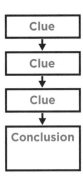

Think and Compare

1. Was Brent Davies's plan a success? Use your Conclusion Map and story details to answer. **Monitor Comprehension: Draw Conclusions**

2. Reread the last paragraph of "Home-Grown Butterflies" on page 396. Why do you think the California students started writing to the students in Costa Rica? **Analyze**

3. What would you change to make Brent Davies's butterfly plan even more successful? **Apply**

4. The people of Barra del Colorado learned how to earn money without **harming** the rain forest. What is the importance of this lesson? Explain your answer. **Evaluate**

5. Read "Save Our Butterflies" on pages 386-387. How is this selection similar to "Home-Grown Butterflies"? How are the two selections different? Use details from both selections in your answer. **Reading/Writing Across Texts**

Poetry

Free Verse Poems do not have any regular pattern of line length, rhyme, meter, or stanzas.

Rhyming Poems use elements such as rhyme and rhythm to express feelings and ideas.

Literary Elements

Personification means human characteristics are given to an animal or thing.

Assonance is the repetition of the same or similar vowel sounds in a series of words.

The phrase "I have waited much longer before" shows the butterfly thinking as a person would.

Monarch Butterfly

Wait I can wait
    For the fullness of wings
    For the lift   For the flight
Wait I can wait
    A moment less
    A moment more
I have waited much longer before
    For the taste of the flower
    For the feel   For the sight
Wait I can wait
    For the prize of the skies
    For the gift of the air
Almost finished
Almost there
    Almost ready
        to rise

— *Marilyn Singer*

The Caterpillar

Brown and furry
Caterpillar in a hurry,
Take your walk
To the shady leaf, or stalk,
    Or what not,
Which may be the chosen spot.
    No toad spy you,

Hovering bird of prey pass
    by you;
Spin and die,
To live again a butterfly.

— *Christina Rossetti*

> "No" and "toad" repeat the long "o" sound to create assonance.

Connect and Compare

1. Find an example of assonance in "Monarch Butterfly." What changes would you make in "The Caterpillar" to include personification? **Apply**

2. What changes would you have to make in order to make "Monarch Butterfly" a rhyming poem? How could you make "The Caterpillar" a free verse poem? **Apply**

3. Which stage in "Home-Grown Butterflies" does "Monarch Butterfly" relate to? **Reading/Writing Across Texts**

 Find out more about free verse and rhyming poems at **www.macmillanmh.com**

401

Writer's Craft

Tone

Writers often use a serious **tone** for scientific topics. Their word choice—for example, using scientific terms and precise adjectives—helps set the tone. A reference book called a *thesaurus* helps writers find the right words.

Write a Magazine Article

Eat Dirt!

by Kamryn G.

Earthworms keep the soil in gardens healthy. How do they do it? One way is by eating dirt. They also eat dead plants, leaves, stems, and even animals. When the worms get rid of their digested food, they add good nutrients to the soil that help plants grow.

The second thing that earthworms do is dig horizontal tunnels in the soil. As they dig, they aerate the soil by turning it over and adding fresh air to it. When the soil is loose, it holds rainwater, and plants can spread their roots and grow.

I used a serious tone to report my research about earthworms.

I used the science word "aerate" to describe what an earthworm does.

Your Turn

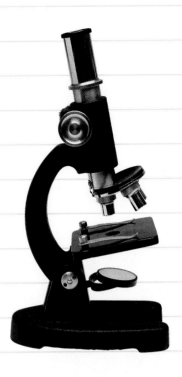

Write a short magazine article of two paragraphs about a science topic. Choose a topic that interests you. Then, do research in magazines, books, or the Internet, with an adult's help. When you write your article, consider using a serious tone. A thesaurus can help you find the right describing words. Use the Writer's Checklist to check your writing.

Writer's Checklist

 Ideas and Content: Did I make my topic clear?

 Organization: Did I organize my information?

 Voice: Did I use a serious **tone** in the article so it tells the facts without showing my feelings?

 Word Choice: Did I use precise adjectives that help the reader understand my topic?

 Sentence Fluency: Did I avoid writing a lot of short and choppy sentences?

 Conventions: Did I use commas correctly? Did I use adjectives and adverbs correctly? Did I check my spelling?

Test Strategy

On My Own

The answer is not in the selection. Form an opinion about what you read to answer questions 4 and 5.

A Change in Plans

by Samantha Gray

Parents hope to replace this old jungle gym with a new one when Wilson School's new playground is built.

The playground at Wilson School has been around for many years. It was just the right size when the school was built. Now the school has many more students, so the playground just isn't big enough anymore.

In October of last year, the Smithville City Council made a promise to build a bigger playground this summer. It will have more swings, slides, and basketball hoops, as well as a modern jungle gym.

Go On ▶

On Monday night, the Wilson School Parents Group learned that the playground will not be finished this summer.

City Council President John Tang told the parents that work will start this summer, but it will take a year for the playground to be built. In the meantime, students will have no playground.

Many parents were upset. They said that students, parents, and school staff have been looking forward to the new playground for a long time.

John Tang explains why the playground will not be built on time.

Why the Plan Changed

During the meeting, one parent spoke up. "Why will it take a whole year to build a simple playground?" she asked.

Mr. Tang said that construction workers are currently working on many projects. They will tear up the old playground over the summer. Then throughout the year they will work on the new playground.

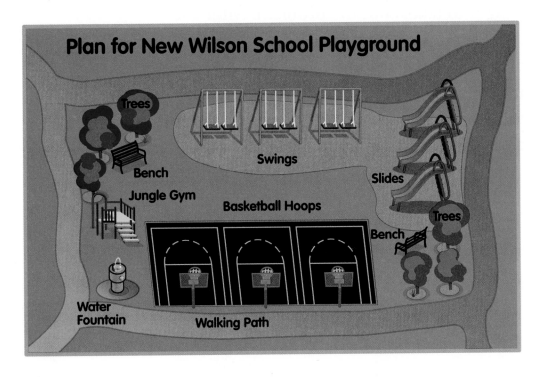

Plan for New Wilson School Playground

Trees
Bench
Jungle Gym
Swings
Slides
Basketball Hoops
Trees
Bench
Water Fountain
Walking Path

Disappointed parents listen to the city council president's speech.

Parents Propose a Solution

The Wilson School Parents Group met again on Tuesday night to talk about the problem. After a few hours, they came up with a solution.

Parents asked the city council to wait until the fall to begin the project. Builders could do the work during the school year. In the meantime, the old playground would still be there for students to use this summer. In addition, parent volunteers would donate their time during the year to help keep the project on schedule.

Go On ▶

Directions: Answer the questions.

1. **What is the theme of this selection?**

   A Playgrounds are a waste of time.
   B Building a playground is not very important.
   C Parents should take charge of school playgrounds.
   D If people work together, they can solve problems.

2. **Why are "Why the Plan Changed" and "Parents Propose a Solution" set apart and in blue letters?**

   A so the reader will stop reading
   B so the reader will know what the next section is about
   C so the reader doesn't have to read the rest of the text
   D so the reader will understand the title

3. **What might the city council have done differently?**

   A spoken to parents as soon as there was a problem
   B ignored parents' wishes
   C asked students to help build the playground
   D cancelled the project

4. **Explain how this article would be written if the theme was "be happy with what you have."**

   Tip

   Form an opinion.

5. **Do you agree with the solution that the parents group presented? Why or why not?**

Writing Prompt

Write a three-paragraph news story about a school event. Answer *who*, *what*, *where*, *when*, and *why*. Make sure each paragraph has a topic sentence and supporting details.

Glossary
What Is a Glossary?

A Glossary can help you find the **meanings** of words in this book that you may not know. The words in the Glossary are listed in **alphabetical order**. **Guide words** at the top of each page tell you the first and last words on the page.

Each word is divided into syllables. The way to pronounce the word is given next. You can understand the pronunciation respelling by using the **pronunciation key** on page 409. A shorter key appears at the bottom of every other page. When a word has more than one syllable, a dark accent mark (´) shows which syllable is stressed. In some words, a light accent mark (´) shows which syllable has a less heavy stress. Sometimes an entry includes a second meaning for the word.

Guide Words

First word on the page   Last word on the page

Sample Entry

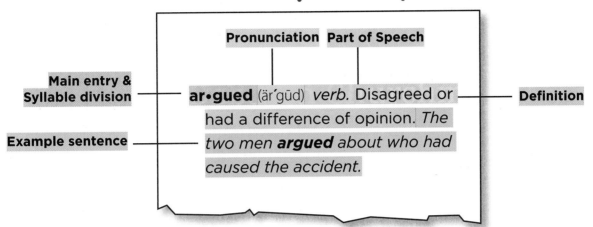

Pronunciation   Part of Speech

Main entry &
Syllable division

ar•gued (är´gŭd) *verb.* Disagreed or had a difference of opinion. *The two men **argued** about who had caused the accident.*

Definition

Example sentence

Pronunciation Key

Phonetic Spelling	Examples
a	at, bad, plaid, laugh
ā	ape, pain, day, break
ä	father, calm
âr	care, pair, bear, their, where
e	end, pet, said, heaven, friend
ē	equal, me, feet, team, piece, key
i	it, big, give, hymn
ī	ice, fine, lie, my
îr	ear, deer, here, pierce
o	odd, hot, watch
ō	old, oat, toe, low
ô	coffee, all, taught, law, fought
ôr	order, fork, horse, story, pour
oi	oil, toy
ou	out, now, bough
u	up, mud, love, double
ū	use, mule, cue, feud, few
ü	rule, true, food, fruit
ù	put, wood, should, look
ûr	burn, hurry, term, bird, word, courage
ə	about, taken, pencil, lemon, circus
b	bat, above, job
ch	chin, such, match

Phonetic Spelling	Examples
d	dear, soda, bad
f	five, defend, leaf, off, cough, elephant
g	game, ago, fog, egg
h	hat, ahead
hw	white, whether, which
j	joke, enjoy, gem, page, edge
k	kite, bakery, seek, tack, cat
l	lid, sailor, feel, ball, allow
m	man, family, dream
n	not, final, pan, knife, gnaw
ng	long, singer
p	pail, repair, soap, happy
r	ride, parent, wear, more, marry
s	sit, aside, pets, cent, pass
sh	shoe, washer, fish, mission, nation
t	tag, pretend, fat, dressed
th	thin, panther, both
th	these, mother, smooth
v	very, favor, wave
w	wet, weather, reward
y	yes, onion
z	zoo, lazy, jazz, rose, dogs, houses
zh	vision, treasure, seizure

Aa

a·chieve (ə chēv´) *verb.* To do or carry out successfully. *Did Thomas **achieve** his goal of cleaning his desk before the bell rang?*

ap·pli·an·ces (ə plī´əns əz) *plural noun.* Small machines or devices that have particular uses, such as toasters, refrigerators, and washing machines. *The store was crowded because of the sale on kitchen **appliances**.*

ar·chi·tects (är´ki tekts´) *plural noun.* People who design buildings and supervise their construction. *A group of **architects** showed up at the empty lot and began planning the building they wanted to make there.*

ar·gued (är´gūd) *verb.* Disagreed or had a difference of opinion. *The two men **argued** about who had caused the accident.*

ar·tist's (är´tists) *possessive noun.* Belonging to a person who is skilled in painting, music, literature, or any other form of art. *The chef uses an **artist's** touch when he puts the toppings on his famous desserts.*

au·to·mat·i·cal·ly (ô´tə mat´ik əl lē) *adverb.* Gets done without a person's control. *Digestion takes place in the body **automatically**.*

Bb

batches (bach´əz) *plural noun.* Groups of things prepared or gathered together. *Tracey and Darryl made several **batches** of cookies for the bake sale at the library.*

beamed (bēmd) *verb.* **1.** Shined brightly. *The sun **beamed** down on the field.* **2.** Smiled brightly. *Marleigh **beamed** when she thought about the joke Raffi told yesterday.*

blos·somed (blos´əmd) *verb.* Grew or developed. *The student kept practicing until she **blossomed** into a wonderful violinist.*

boast·ing (bōst´ing) *verb.* Talking with too much pride. *Everyone got annoyed when Lisa started **boasting** about her new bicycle.*

busi·ness (biz´nis) *noun.* **1.** The work a person does to earn a living. *Kenneth worked in the fashion **business** for eight years.* **2.** The buying and selling of things; trade. *The kite shop does good **business** in the summer.*

Cc

cap·ture (kap´chər) *verb.* To catch and hold a person, animal, or thing. *The park rangers were trying to **capture** the bear that was roaming the picnic area.*

clumps (klumps) *plural noun.* Groups or clusters. *After Jennifer went swimming, she had **clumps** of knots in her long hair.*

com·bine (kəm bīn´) *verb.* To join together; unite. *We will **combine** eggs, flour, and milk to make batter for pancakes.*

com·mu·ni·ty (kə mū´ni tē) *noun.* **1.** A group of people who live together in the same place. *Our **community** voted to build a new library.* **2.** A group of people who share a common interest. *The scientific **community** is involved in important research projects.*

con·flict (kon´flikt) *noun.* A strong disagreement. *The school board is in **conflict** with the mayor's office about where to build the playground.*

con·struc·tion (kən struk´shən) *noun.* The act or process of building something. *It was interesting to watch the **construction** of the new grocery store.*

con·tain (kən tān´) *verb.* To hold inside. *The storage boxes **contain** clothes.*

at; āpe; fär; câre; end; mē; it; īce; pîerce; hot; ōld; sông; fôrk; oil; out; up; ūse; rüle; pùll; tûrn; chin; sing; shop; thin; this; hw in white; zh in treasure.

The symbol ə stands for the unstressed vowel sound in about, taken, pencil, lemon, and circus.

Gg

ge·o·met·ric (jē′ə met′rik) *adjective.*
1. Consisting of or decorated with lines, angles, circles, triangles, or similar shapes. *The rug in my bedroom has a* **geometric** *design of blue circles and yellow squares.* **2.** Having to do with geometry. *A cone is a* **geometric** *shape.*

gift (gift) *noun.* Something given to someone, such as a present. *Nigel received a special* **gift** *on his birthday.*

grace (grās) *noun.* Beautiful movement, or style. *The dancer moved with* **grace** *on the stage.*

grown·ups (grōn′ups) *plural noun.* Adults. *The children were playing games while the* **grownups** *prepared the dessert.*

grum·bled (grum′bəld) *verb.* Complained in a low voice. *The class* **grumbled** *when the teacher gave them a lot of homework to do over the holiday.*

Hh

harm·ing (härm′ing) *verb.* Doing damage to or hurting. *The construction company was told that it was* **harming** *the environment because it cut down so many trees.*

his·tor·i·cal (hi stôr′i kəl) *adjective.* Having to do with history. *This book contains* **historical** *information, such as how our town began and who its leaders have been.*

hives (hīvz) *plural noun.* Boxes or houses for bees to live in. *We were warned to stay away from the bee* **hives** *that were in the park.*

Ii

im·age (im´ij) *noun.* A picture of a person or thing. *I still have an **image** in my head of the beautiful sunset at the beach.*

Word History

Image comes from the Latin *imago*, or *imitari*, "to imitate."

in·di·vid·u·al (in´də vij´ü əl) *adjective.* Single; separate. *The coffee was served with **individual** packets of sugar.*

in·flu·enced (in´flü ənst) *verb.* Had an effect on, especially by giving suggestions or by serving as an example. *The older members of my family **influenced** me in many ways when I was growing up.*

in·gre·di·ent (in grē´dē ənt) *noun.* Any one of the parts used in a recipe or mixture. *The baker was missing one **ingredient** for making a cake.*

in·ter·rupt·ed (in´tə rup´təd) *verb.* Broke in upon or stopped something or someone. *A loud car alarm **interrupted** our teacher from speaking.*

in·ter·viewed (in´tər vūd´) *verb.* Obtained information from someone by asking questions. *Last night my favorite actress was **interviewed** on television.*

in·volved (in volvd´) *adjective.* Taken up with. *Many students said that they wanted to become **involved** in raising money for the park.*

Kk

kind·heart·ed (kīnd´här´tid) *adjective.* Having or showing a friendly or gentle nature. *The **kindhearted** woman put food outside her house for birds to eat during the winter.*

Ll

leak·y (lē´kē) *adjective.* Having a hole or small opening that water, light, or air can pass through. *The **leaky** hose caused a big puddle whenever I tried to water the plants.*

lone·some (lōn´səm) *adjective.* Not often visited by people; deserted. *The **lonesome** house in the swamp was a sad sight.*

---

at; āpe; fär; câre; end; mē; it; īce; pîerce; hot; ōld; sông; fôrk; oil; out; up; ūse; rüle; pùll; tûrn; chin; sing; shop; thin; <u>th</u>is; hw in white; zh in treasure.

The symbol ə stands for the unstressed vowel sound in about, taken, pencil, lemon, and circus.

luck·i·est (luk´ē est´) *adjective.* Having or bringing the most good luck. *Of all the contest winners, James was the* **luckiest**; *he won the grand prize.*

Mm

mag·nif·i·cent (mag nif´ə sənt) *adjective.* Very beautiful and grand. *We walked through the* **magnificent** *garden and admired all the beautiful flowers.*

mar·mo·sets (mär´mə zetz´) *plural noun.* Small, tropical monkeys with claws, soft thick fur, tufted ears, and long tails. *Michael enjoyed watching the* **marmosets** *at play.*

mas·ter·piece (mas´tər pēs´) *noun.* **1.** A great work of art. *The painting* Mona Lisa *by Da Vinci is thought to be a* **masterpiece**. **2.** Something done with great skill. *Her plan to surprise her brother on his birthday was a* **masterpiece**.

marmoset

Nn

na·tive (nā´tiv) *adjective.* Originally living or growing in a region or country. *The cheetah is* **native** *to sub-Saharan Africa.*

need·y (nē´dē) *adjective.* Very poor; not having enough to live on. *Food and clothing were donated to* **needy** *families in the area.*

news·pa·per (nüz´pā´pər) *noun.* A publication printed on sheets of paper that contain news and are published every day or every week. *Many people read the* **newspaper** *every morning on the way to work.*

numb (num) *adjective.* Lacking feelings. *The members of the basketball team were* **numb** *after they lost the championship game.*

Oo

of·fi·cial (ə fish´əl) *adjective.* Coming from or approved by authority. *The referee announced the* **official** *score of the basketball game.*

or·gan·i·za·tion (ôr´gə ni zā´shən) *noun.* A group of people joined together for a specific purpose. *Her father joined a business* **organization**.

o·rig·i·nal (ərij´ənəl) *adjective.* **1.** Made, done, thought of, or used for the first time; new. *There are not many **original** ideas coming out of Hollywood anymore.* **2.** Able to do, make, or think of something new or different. *One doesn't need to be an **original** thinker to watch television.* **3.** Relating to or belonging to the origin or beginning of something; first. *The **original** owners moved out of the house years ago.*

own·ers (ō´nərz) *plural noun.* People who possess something. *Sarah was very proud that the knitting shop was doing well because she was one of the **owners**.*

Pp

per·son·al·i·ty (pûr´sənal´i tē) *noun.* All the qualities, traits, habits, and behavior of a person. *It was in her **personality** to always be cheerful.*

pit·i·ful (pit´i fəl) *adjective.* Making people feel sorrow for. *The boy standing outside in the cold without his coat looked **pitiful**.*

pos·ses·sions (pəzesh´ənz) *plural noun.* Things that are owned by someone. *Many of his **possessions** were stolen by thieves who broke into his house.*

pow·ered (pou´ərd) *verb.* Filled with the energy to function or operate. *The toy truck was **powered** by batteries.*

pre·served (pri zûrvd´) *verb.* Protected; kept from harm. *The refrigerator door was closed so that the food's freshness could be **preserved**.*

pride (prīd) *noun.* **1.** A person's feeling of self-respect, dignity, and self-worth. *Although Rhonda did not score an A in science class, she never lost her sense of **pride**.* **2.** A company of lions. *The antelope were startled by a small **pride** moving in their direction.*

---

at; āpe; fär; câre; end; mē; it; īce; pîerce; hot; ōld; sông; fôrk; oil; out; up; ūse; rüle; pùll; tûrn; chin; sing; shop; thin; this; hw in white; zh in treasure.

The symbol ə stands for the unstressed vowel sound in about, taken, pencil, lemon, and circus.

pro·duce (prə düs′ *for verb;* prō′düs *for noun*) *verb.* To make or create something. *The class was asked to* **produce** *a play about the signing of the Declaration of Independence.* noun. Farm products, such as fruits and vegetables. *Mom likes to buy fresh* **produce** *from the farmer's market.*

profits (prof′its) *plural noun.* Amounts of money earned on sales. *The difference in* **profits** *that winter between the two shops was small.*

pro·tect (prə tekt′) *verb.* To defend from harm. *Mr. Trang put on a heavy overcoat to* **protect** *himself from the cold.*

pur·chased (pûr′chəst) *verb.* Got something by paying money for it. *Lester's mother* **purchased** *a bicycle to give to him for his birthday.*

Qq

quar·rel·ing (kwôr′əl ing′) *verb.* Having a heated argument. *My uncles were always* **quarreling** *about which baseball team was better.*

Rr

rebuild (rē bild′) *verb.* To build again or repair. *The farmer wanted to* **rebuild** *his shed after the storm blew it down.*

rec·i·pes (res′ə pēz) *plural noun.* Lists of ingredients and instructions for making something to eat or drink. *My mother has many cookie* **recipes***.*

rent (rent) *noun.* A payment for the use of something. *The* **rent** *for the house was more than he was willing to pay.* verb. **1.** To get the right to use something in return for payment. *Katie and Jill planned to* **rent** *an apartment together once they finished college.* **2.** To give the right to use something in return for payment. *The landlord wanted to* **rent** *out the apartment to a quiet tenant.*

re·quire·ments (ri kwīr´mənts) *plural noun.* Things that are necessary; demands or needs. *There were certain **requirements** the students had to meet before they could move on to the next grade.*

re·search (rē´sûrch, ri sûrch´) *noun.* A careful study or investigation in order to learn facts. *A lot of **research** had to be done before the paper could be written.*

Word History

The Old French *recerchier*, which means "to search closely," is where the word **research** comes from.

re·solve (ri zolv´) *verb.* To settle, explain, or solve. *Barry can **resolve** the situation by offering to pay for anything that has been broken.*

re·spect (ri spekt´) *verb.* To have or show honor or consideration. *It is important to **respect** the opinions of others, even if you don't agree with everything they say.*

re·treats (ri trēts´) *verb.* Goes back or withdraws, as from danger. *A tigress **retreats** when it realizes it is outnumbered. plural noun.* Places to go to for safety, peace, and comfort. *Staying in **retreats** was a helpful way for Bob to leave his problems behind him.*

ru·ined (rü´ind) *verb.* Damaged greatly or harmed. *The flood **ruined** all our carpets in the basement.*

Ss

sched·ule (skej´ül, əl) *noun.* A list of times, events, or things to do. *He checked his **schedule** to make sure he would be available.*

Word History

Schedule has a long history: starting with the Greek *skhida*, "to split"; the Latin *scida*, "papyrus strip"; the Old French *cedule*, and Middle English *sedule*, which both mean "slip of parchment" or "paper, note."

at; āpe; fär; câre; end; mē; it; īce; pîerce; hot; ōld; sông; fôrk; oil; out; up; ūse; rüle; pull; tûrn; chin; sing; shop; thin; this; hw in white; zh in treasure.

The symbol ə stands for the unstressed vowel sound in about, taken, pencil, lemon, and circus.

school·house (skül´hous´) *noun.* A building used as a school. *On Friday night, a dance was held at the* **schoolhouse**.

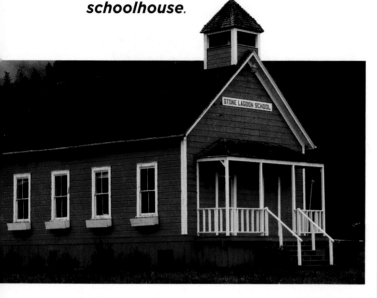

scram·bled (skram´bəld) *verb.* Moved or climbed quickly. *We all* **scrambled** *to the finish line in the three-legged race.*

screamed (skrēmd) *verb.* Made a loud cry or sound. *The woman* **screamed** *when she saw her baby crawling close to the pool.*

seized (sēzd) *verb.* Took hold of or grabbed. *The guard* **seized** *the money out of the thief's hand.*

sep·a·rate (sep´ə rāt´) *verb.* To set apart or place apart. *After the big fight, we had to* **separate** *the cat and the dog and put them in different rooms.*

se·quence (sē´kwəns) *noun.* **1.** The coming of one thing after another in a fixed order. *The* **sequence** *of even numbers from one to ten is 2, 4, 6, 8, 10.* **2.** A series of connected things. *A* **sequence** *of drawings showed the figure moving from left to right.*

ser·vi·ces (sûr´vis əz´) *plural noun.* A variety of tasks or acts done for others, usually for pay. *The car wash provided other* **services**, *such as dusting and vacuuming inside the car.*

shal·low (shal´ō) *adjective.* Not deep. *All the young children were playing in the* **shallow** *part of the pool.*

shel·ter (shel´tər) *noun.* Something that covers or protects. *Once it began to rain, the group immediately looked for* **shelter**.

should·n't (shud´ent) *verb.* Contraction of should not. *You* **shouldn't** *run with scissors in your hands.*

shud·dered (shud´ərd) *verb.* Trembled suddenly. *The house* **shuddered** *during the earthquake.*

side·walks (sīd´wôkz´) *plural noun.* Paths by the side of the street or road, usually made of cement. *Vladimir and Bill were paid to shovel snow off the* **sidewalks** *around their apartment building.*

sleek (slēk) *adjective.* Looking healthy and well cared for. *Everyone admired the **sleek** poodle at the dog show.*

slee·py (slē′pē) *adjective.* Ready for or needing sleep. *After a big dinner, Raymond felt very **sleepy** and sat down on the couch.*

slo·gan (slō′gən) *noun.* A phrase, statement, or motto. *Today our teacher asked us to think up a **slogan** for our science club.*

sprout (sprout) *verb.* To begin to grow. *Maria was pleased to see that the sunflower seeds she planted were finally beginning to **sprout**.* *noun.* A new growth on a plant; bud or shoot. *There was a **sprout** on the plant that would soon become a leaf.*

stor·age (stôr′ij) *noun.* A place for keeping things for future use. *Mr. Chen used his garage mainly for **storage**.*

strolled (strōld) *verb.* Walked in a slow, relaxed manner. *The tourists **strolled** through the streets looking at all the big buildings and store windows.*

struc·tures (struk′chərz) *plural noun.* Things that are built, such as buildings. *From so far away, the **structures** on the horizon were hard to make out.*

Word History

Structure comes from the Latin word *struere*, which means "to construct."

stur·dy (stûr′dē) *adjective.* Strong or solid. *The new table is very **sturdy**, and we are able to put many heavy boxes on it.*

sup·ply (sə plī′) *noun.* An amount of something needed or available for use. *We had a **supply** of candles and batteries in the closet in case of an emergency.*

---

at; āpe; fär; câre; end; mē; it; īce; pîerce; hot; ōld; sông; fôrk; oil; out; up; ūse; rüle; pùll; tûrn; chin; sing; shop; thin; **th**is; hw in white; zh in treasure.

The symbol ə stands for the unstressed vowel sound in about, taken, pencil, lemon, and circus.

sway (swā) *verb.* To move or swing back and forth or side to side. *The trees began to gently* ***sway*** *in the tropical wind.*

Tt

tast·y (tās′tē) *adjective.* Having a pleasant flavor. *The freshly baked brownies were very* ***tasty***.

tend (tend) *verb.* To look after or take care of something. *It was the farmer's job to* ***tend*** *to the cows and chickens and make sure they had enough food.*

thrilled (thrild) *verb.* Filled with pleasure or excitement. *The team members were* ***thrilled*** *when they heard their best player was not badly injured.*

tour (tŭr) *noun.* A trip or journey in which many places are visited or many things are seen. *The guide led a* ***tour*** *through the museum and explained all the famous artwork.*

trad·ers (trā′dərz) *plural noun.* People who buy and sell things as a business. *The* ***traders*** *went to the settlers to sell them blankets and clothes.*

Vv

vol·un·teers (vol′ən tîrz′) *plural noun.* People who offer to do things by choice and often without pay. *Several* ***volunteers*** *showed up to help clean up the park and paint the fence.*

Ww

wailed (wāld) *verb.* Made a long and sad cry, especially to show grief or pain. *The baby* ***wailed*** *when she dropped her toy.*

Yy

ya·poks (yə poks′) *plural noun.* Tropical aquatic opossums with dense fur, webbed feet, and long tails. *The young* ***yapoks*** *huddled together beneath the shade of the palm tree.*

yearned (yûrnd) *verb.* Felt a strong and deep desire. *The school team* ***yearned*** *for the chance to play.*

Acknowledgments

The publisher gratefully acknowledges permission to reprint the following copyrighted material:

"Animal Homes" by Ann O. Squire. Copyright © 2001 by Children's Press®, a Division of Scholastic Inc. All rights reserved. Reprinted by permission.

"Beatrice's Goat" by Page McBrier, illustrations by Lori Lohstoeter. Text copyright © 2001 by Page McBrier. Illustrations copyright © 2001 by Lori Lohstoeter. Reprinted by permission of Atheneum Books for Young Readers, an imprint of Simon & Schuster Children's Publishing Division.

"Boom Town" by Sonia Levitin, illustrations by Cat Bowman Smith. Text copyright © 1998 by Sonia Levitin. Illustrations copyright © 1998 by Cat Bowman Smith. Reprinted with permission by Orchard Books a Grolier Company.

"A Castle on Viola Street" by DyAnne DiSalvo. Copyright © 2001 by DyAnne DiSalvo. Reprinted with permission of HarperCollins Children's Books, a division of HarperCollins Publishers.

"The Caterpillar" by Christina Rossetti from BOOK OF POEMS by Tomie dePaola. Text copyright © 1988 by Tomie dePaola. Reprinted with permission.

"A Child's Call to Aid the Zoo" by Jim Davis. Copyright © 2003 by Jim Davis. Reprinted with permission by The Fresno Bee, a division of the The McClatchy Company.

"Cook-a-Doodle Doo!" by Janet Stevens and Susan Stevens Crummel, illustrations by Janet Stevens. Text copyright © 1999 by Janet Stevens and Susan Stevens Crummel. Illustrations copyright © 1999 by Janet Stevens. Reprinted with permission of Harcourt Brace & Company.

"Home Sweet Home" by John Ciardi from THE HOPEFUL TROUT AND OTHER LIMERICKS by John Ciardi. Text copyright © 1989 by Myra J. Ciardi. Reprinted with permission by Houghton Mifflin Company.

"Home-Grown Butterflies" by Deborah Churchman from RANGER RICK®. Copyright © 1998 by National Wildlife Federation. Reprinted with permission of the National Wildlife Federation, May 1998.

"Monarch Butterfly" by Marilyn Singer from FIREFLIES AT MIDNIGHT by Marilyn Singer. Text copyright © 2003 by Marilyn Singer. Reprinted with permission by Atheneum Books for Young Readers, an imprint of Simon & Schuster Children's Publishing Division.

"Mother to Tigers" by George Ella Lyon, illustrations by Peter Catalanotto. Text copyright © 2003 by George Ella Lyon. Illustrations copyright © 2003 by Peter Catalanotto. Reprinted by permission of Atheneum Books for Young Readers, an imprint of Simon & Schuster Children's Publishing Division.

"My Very Own Room" by Amada Irma Pérez, illustrations by Maya Christina Gonzalez. Text copyright © 2000 by Amada Irma Pérez. Illustrations copyright © 2000 by Maya Christina Gonzalez. Reprinted with permission by Children's Book Press.

"The Printer" by Myron Uhlberg, illustrations by Henri Sørensen. Text copyright © 2003 Myron Uhlberg. Illustrations copyright © 2003 by Henri Sørensen. Reprinted with permission of Peachtree Publishers.

"Seven Spools of Thread: A Kwanzaa Story" by Angela Shelf Medearis, illustrations by Daniel Minter. Text copyright © 2000 by Angela Shelf Medearis. Illustrations copyright © 2000 by Daniel Minter. Reprinted with permission by Albert Whitman & Company.

"Think of darkness" by David McCord from MORE RHYMES OF THE NEVER WAS AND ALWAYS IS by David McCord. Copyright © 1979, 1980 by David McCord. Reprinted with permission of Little, Brown and Company (Canada) Limited.

"Wilbur's Boast" (from "CHARLOTTE'S WEB") by E. B. White, illustrations by Garth Williams. Text copyright © 1952 by E. B. White. Text copyright © renewed 1980 by E. B. White. Illustrations copyright © renewed 1980 by Estate of Garth Williams. Reprinted with permission by HarperCollins Publishers, a division of HarperCollins Publishers.

ILLUSTRATIONS
Cover Illustration: Scott Gustafson

12-13: Shane McGowan. 14-39: Janet Stevens. 44: Tim Johnson. 50-73: Daniel Minter. 76: Tim Johnson. 83: Rick Nease for TFK. 84: Jack Thomas. 108-109: Traci Van Wagoner. 110: Tim Johnson. 116-139: Maya Christina Gonzalez. 142: Wetzel & Company. 144: Tim Johnson. 146-149: Wetzel & Company. 154-177: Cat Bowman Smith. 180: Wetzel & Company. 182: Tim Johnson. 188-211: Lori Lohstoeter. 216: Tim Johnson. 221: (tl) Topham/The Image Works. 222: (cr) Mario Ruiz/Time Life Pictures/Getty Images. 234-253: Henri Sørensen. 255: Robert Schuster. 258: Tim Johnson. 282-283: Amy Ning. 284: Tim Johnson. 294-315: DyAnne DiSalvo. 320: Tim Johnson. 326-338: Garth Williams. 344: Tim Johnson. 354: Library of Congress, Prints & Photographs Division. 362-379: Peter Catalanotto. 380-381: Nicole Rutten. 382: (bc) Tim Johnson. 402: Tim Johnson. 405: Joe Taylor. 408-409: Lindy Burnett.

PHOTOGRAPHY
All Photographs are by Macmillan/McGraw Hill (MMH) except as noted below:

10-11: (bkgd) © Gabe Palmer/CORBIS. 11: (inset) C Squared Studios/Getty Images. 38: Courtesy Susan Stevens Crummel. 40: Comstock/Alamy. 41: Premium Stock/CORBIS. 42: (tl) Foodpix/Getty Images; (br) Royalty Free/CORBIS. 43: Steve Niedorf Photography/The Image Bank/Getty Images. 44: (bkgd) Wetzel&Company; (b) Michael Newman/Photo Edit Inc. 45: Judd Pilossof/FoodPix/Getty Images. 46-47: (bkgd) © James Marshall/CORBIS. 47: (inset) Royalty-Free/CORBIS. 48: (t) Myrleen Ferguson Cate/Photo Edit Inc; (bl) Richard Hutchings/Photo Edit Inc. 49: Myrleen Ferguson Cate/Photo Edit Inc. 72: (tcl) Courtesy Angela Meaderis; (cr) Courtesy Daniel Minter. 74: Tom & Dee Ann McCarthy/CORBIS. 75: Ellen Senisi/The Image Works. 76: Royalty-Free/CORBIS. 77: (tl) Tom McCarthy/Photo Edit Inc; (tc) Emma Lee/LifeFile Photos Ltd./Alamy; (tr) Photodisc/Getty Images. 78: (bl) Peter Lillie/OSF/Animals Animals; (br) Wolfgang Kaehler/CORBIS. 78-79: (t) Michael Gadomski/Animals Animals. 79: (bl) David Hall/Photo Researchers; (br) Doug Wechsler/Animals Animals. 80: Barry Iverson for TFK. 81: (tl) Don Enger/Animals Animals; (tr) W. Perry Conway/CORBIS; (tcl) Nature's Images/Photo Researchers; (tcr) S. Michael Bisceglie/Animals Animals; (cl) Gregory Ochocki/Photo Researchers; (cr) Nigel Dennis/APBL/Animals Animals; (bcr) Photolink/Photodisc/Getty Images; (bl) Stephanie Harvin. 82: Jack Thomas. 83: Joel W. Rogers/CORBIS. 85: Jack Thomas. 86: (cl) Tom Myers/Photo Researchers; (bl) Courtesy Jean Mahoney. 88: SuperStock/AGE Fotostock. 89: (bkgd) Dian Lofton for TFK. 89: (c) Burke/Triolo Productions/Brand X/Alamy. (cr) Tracy Montana/PhotoLink/Getty Images; (bkgd) Ben Osborne/Getty Images. 91: (inset) Photodisc/Getty Images. 92: (bl) ©Peter Kaplan/Photo Researchers. 92-93: (t) ©Nancy Rotenberg/Animals Animals/Earth Scenes. 93: Heifer International. 94: (bc) ©Robert Cranston/RJ's Images of Nature. 94-95: (bkgd) Wetzel & Company. 95: (c) Darrell Wong/The Fresno Bee. 96: (bc) Courtesy Stacey L. Caha. 96-97: (bkgd) Wetzel & Company. 97: (bc) Courtesy of The Fresno Bee. 98: (bl) Courtesy Stacey L. Caha. 98-99: (bkgd) Wetzel & Company. 99: (tc) ©Robert Cranston/RJ's Images of Nature. 100: (tc) David Hunter/The Fresno Bee. 100-101: (bkgd) Wetzel & Company. 101: (bc) Courtesy Stacey L. Caha. 102: (bc) Courtesy Stacey L. Caha. 102-103: (bkgd) Wetzel & Company. 103: (tc) Courtesy Stacey L. Caha. 104: (tc) Courtesy Stacey L. Caha. 104-105: (bkgd) Wetzel & Company. 105: (bc) ©Robert